Super Simple
Cupcake
Recipes

Cookbook Resources, LLC
Highland Village, Texas

Super Simple Cupcake Recipes

Printed August 2010

© Copyright 2010 by Cookbook Resources, LLC

International Standard Book Number: 978-1-59769-046-1

Library of Congress Control Number:

Library of Congress Cataloging-in-Publication Data

Cover and illustrations by Razer Designs and Nancy Bohanan

Edited, Designed, Published and Manufactured in the United States of America
by Cookbook Resources, LLC
541 Doubletree Drive
Highland Village, Texas 75077

Toll free 866-229-2665

www.cookbookresources.com

cookbook resources LLC
Bringing Family and Friends to the Table

Simply FUN!

What about exciting games right in the middle of your kitchen? That's right and it's loads of fun!

Make some easy cupcakes with the recipes in this cookbook, invite your friends over and decorate each cupcake. You can create original works of art! (Then eat them!)

There are plenty of reasons to make cupcakes... you are bored... your brother is hungry... your sister is hungry... you want something sweet... you want to be creative... you want to learn how to bake... Get the idea? Any reason you can think of is a good enough reason to make cupcakes!

How creative are you?

Get ready... and have some fun!

This is your easy introduction to *Super Simple Cupcake Recipes*... CHOOSE YOUR RECIPE!!!

Continued next page...

Continued from previous page...

Step One: Make a list, go to the grocery store and buy the ingredients, decorations and paper cupcake liners you will need (if they are not already in the pantry and/or refrigerator).

Step Two: Line up the ingredients on the kitchen counter. Line up the utensils, bowls and muffin pans you will use.

Step Three: Follow the directions in the recipe. Pour batter into paper liners in muffin or cupcake pan. Place cupcakes in preheated oven and bake according to the directions.

Step Four: Clean up your mess while cupcakes bake and cool. Get ready to decorate your treasures.

Step Five: Decorate your delicious cupcakes any way you want. You are the genius! Now... eat them all within a couple of days. (They're always the best right after you make them.)

Have a great time!

Contents

Contents

Any Day – Everyday Cupcakes...continued

Contents

Contents

Frostings, Icings and More...continued

Bonus Section: EASY CAKES! 217

Contents

Dedication

Cookbook Resources' mission is

Bringing Family and Friends to the Table.

We recognize the importance of shared meals as a means of building family bonds with memories and traditions that will last a lifetime. At mealtimes we share more than food. We share ourselves.

This cookbook is dedicated with gratitude and respect to all those who show their love by making home-cooked meals and bringing family and friends to the table.

Decorating Ideas

There are literally thousands of ideas that make decorating fun, exciting and very creative. You can probably think of more things than we can come up with, but just to get you started, here are some great ideas.

Edible Decorations:

- Frostings and icings
- Food colors: liquids, oils, pastes, gels and powders
- Sprinkles
- Nonpareils (shiny little candy balls)
- Meringues: Mountain peaks at ski resort, Santa's beard, snow
- Candies: Facial features, borders for roads, ski slopes or paths, mountains, Indian tepees, rainbows
- Chocolate chips (all sizes)
- Chocolate shavings (dark chocolate and white chocolate): White caps on water, clouds
- Cookies and cookie crumbs
- Sugars: brown, granulated, powdered
- Chow mein noodles
- Fruits and veggies
- Nuts
- Flaked coconut

- Spices: cinnamon
- Fresh herbs-mint and parsley leaves
- Cinnamon sticks
- Honey
- Sauces: caramel, fudge, chocolate
- Pie fillings
- Marshmallows
- Edible glitter, sugars and sprinkles
- Fillings
- Dragees and edible pearls
- Ice cream cones

Non-Edible Decorations:

- Cupcake paper liners, foils, wraps
- Stencils
- Candy molds
- Cupcake and muffin pans
- Cookie cutters
- Ribbons
- Candles
- Small toys
- Cake toppers
- Beads
- Ice cream sticks
- Toothpicks
- Flowers
- Stationery and monograms
- Decorative trays, towers, stands and plates (or create your own with wrapping paper/ stationery and cardboard boxes)

Quick Tips for Cupcakes

1. **Read the entire recipe.** Make sure you have the ingredients and utensils, pans, etc. you need.

2. **Let ingredients come to room temperature.**

   - It takes about 20 to 30 minutes for eggs. A stick of butter takes about 60 minutes. Measure milk and let it set in the measuring cup.

   - *Want it faster?* Place eggs in a bowl of warm (not hot) water and dry them off when ready to crack. Slice or grate cold butter onto a plate and set it over a bowl of warm water for about 10 minutes.

3. **Proper measuring is very important.**

   - For dry ingredients, spoon lightly into measuring cup, overfilling the top. Level the top with the edge of a spatula or knife.

   - Brown sugar should be packed firmly into measuring cups and then leveled.

   - For liquid ingredients, use glass measuring cups. Pour to the exact level needed. (Look at it at eye level.)

4. **Use large eggs for baking.** If separating eggs, separate them while they are cold; then let whites and yolks come to room temperature.

5. **Once you begin mixing, complete making the batter, pour it in the paper liners and place in the preheated oven immediately.** The cupcakes will not be as good if the batter sits around before baking.

6. **Always set the timer for the shortest baking time shown**; check for doneness at that time. Bake for additional minutes if needed. When a toothpick inserted in the center of a cupcake comes out clean (or with a just a few dry crumbs), the cupcakes are done.

   Keep in mind that the smaller the cupcake, the quicker it will cook. The longer it bakes, the drier it will be.

7. **Let cupcakes cool completely before frosting,** otherwise the frosting will soften and slip off.

 This Icon indicates recipes which use mixes.

The 10 Most Popular Flavors of Cupcakes:
1. Chocolate and Vanilla
2. Red Velvet
3. Carrot Cake
4. Peanut Butter
5. Lemon
6. Chocolate
7. Coffee
8. Banana
9. Pumpkin
10. Vanilla

Easiest
of the
Easy

Easy Basic Cupcakes

½ cup shortening
1 cup sugar
3 eggs
1¾ cups flour
2 teaspoons baking powder
½ cup milk
1 teaspoon vanilla

1. Preheat oven to 350°.

2. Cream shortening, sugar and eggs together until light and fluffy.

3. Sift flour, baking powder and ½ teaspoon salt and add alternately with milk to creamed mixture.

4. Add vanilla. Beat thoroughly. Pour into paper liners in cupcake pans.

5. Bake for 15 to 20 minutes. Yields 18 cupcakes.

Decorations:

1 (12 ounce) container ready-to-
   serve vanilla frosting
1 (10 ounce) container prepared
   cake icing

1. Spread cupcakes with vanilla frosting using icing spatula or back of spoon.

2. Draw your favorite designs on each cupcake using cake icing in a squeezable tube with small nozzle tip.

Why did the little cupcake major in hotel and restaurant management?
   Because it wanted to be a hostess.

Butter Pecan Cupcakes

1 (18 ounce) box butter-pecan
   cake mix
⅓ cup canola oil
3 eggs, slightly beaten
½ cup finely chopped pecans

1. Preheat oven to 350°.

2. Beat cake mix, 1 cup water and beaten eggs
    in bowl for 2 minutes on low speed. Stir
    in pecans.

3. Pour two-thirds batter into 24 muffin cups
    with paper linings and bake for 22 to
    25 minutes or until toothpick inserted in
    center comes out clean.

Glaze:

1 tablespoon butter, softened
2 tablespoons maple syrup
⅓ cup powdered sugar
¼ cup very finely chopped pecans

1. Combine butter, maple syrup and powdered sugar in bowl and beat thoroughly.

2. Stir in pecans and drizzle over hot cupcakes.

Cooking times and the number each recipe makes will vary based on the muffin pan used, how much batter is in each cup, additions of nuts and raisins, and altitude.

Children's Cupcake Cones

1 (9 ounce) package chocolate
    cake mix
3 eggs
⅓ cup canola oil
1 (12 count) box ice cream cones
    with flat bottoms

1. Preheat oven to 350°.

2. Prepare cake batter according to package
   directions with eggs, oil and 1¼ cups water.

3. Pour 3 tablespoons batter into ice cream
   cones to fill about half full.

4. Set cones in muffin cups and bake for
   25 to 30 minutes. (These should rise to
   top of cones). Cool.

Decorations:

**1 (12 ounce) container frosting of
your choice**

1. Stir the frosting in a bowl. Frost cupakes the
easy way by dipping the top in the frosting
and swirling.

Hostess CupCakes were first made in
1919, but they were just a small snack cake.
It wasn't until 1950 when they were filled
with a crème center that they became the
Hostess CupCakes of today.

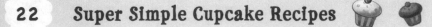
Chocolate-Peanut Butter Yummies

1 (21 ounce) package double fudge
    brownie mix
2 eggs
3 (9 ounce) packages miniature
    peanut butter cups

1. Preheat oven to 350°.

2. Prepare brownie mix according to package directions using 2 eggs. Spoon into 8 miniature foil cupcake liners and fill three-fourths full.

3. Place peanut butter cup in center of each and push into batter. Bake for 20 to 25 minutes or until toothpick inserted in center comes out clean. Yields 8 cupcakes.

Decorations:

1 (16 ounce) container ready-to-
     serve buttercream frosting
½ cup peanut butter
1 (2 ounce) jar chocolate sprinkles
½ cup peanuts
Miniature peanut butter cups

1. Place buttercream frosting in small bowl, stir in peanut butter and mix well. Spread frosting generously over cupcakes.

2. Turn cupcake on its side and roll edge in chocolate sprinkles. Place peanuts in frosting and top with peanut butter cup halves.

Fun Cupcakes

1 (18 ounce) box white cake mix
⅓ cup canola oil
3 eggs, beaten
30 flat-bottom ice cream cones

1. Preheat oven to 325°.

2. Prepare cake mix according to package directions using oil, eggs and 1 cup water in bowl.

3. Place ice cream cones in muffin cups on baking sheet and fill each cone a scant two-thirds full with batter.

4. Bake for 25 to 30 minutes and cool completely before frosting.

Decorations:

1 (16 ounce) container confetti
    frosting
½ cup fruit Skittles® candies

1. Frost each fun cake with confetti frosting
    and sprinkle about 3 to 5 Skittles® on top of
    each cupcake.

*Vegetables are a must on a diet. I suggest
carrot cake, zucchini bread, and pumpkin pie.*
Jim Davis, Garfield

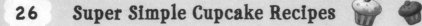

 # In-Your-Face Cupcakes

**1 (18 ounce) box classic white
   cake mix
⅓ cup canola oil
3 eggs, slightly beaten**

1. Preheat oven to 350°.

2. Blend cake mix, oil, eggs and 1 cup water in bowl and beat at low speed for 2 minutes.

3. Place paper liners into 18 muffin cups and spoon mixture two-thirds full into each cup.

4. Bake for 20 minutes and test for doneness. Remove from oven and cool cupcakes on wire rack.

Decorations:

**1 (16 ounce) container buttercream
    frosting
Mini candy-coated chocolate candies**

1. Spread buttercream frosting over each
   cupcake and make a "face" with candy
   eyes, nose and a big smile. Place on
   doily-lined plate.

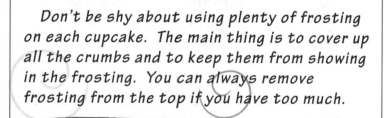

*Don't be shy about using plenty of frosting
on each cupcake. The main thing is to cover up
all the crumbs and to keep them from showing
in the frosting. You can always remove
frosting from the top if you have too much.*

Sour Cream Cupcakes

1 tablespoon shortening
1 cup sugar
2 eggs
½ teaspoon baking soda
½ cup sour cream
1½ cups flour
½ teaspoon cream of tartar
⊠ teaspoon mace

1. Preheat oven to 350°.

2. Cream shortening, sugar and eggs together until light and fluffy. Dissolve baking soda in sour cream.

3. Sift flour, 1½ teaspoons salt, cream of tartar and mace together and add alternately with sour cream to first mixture. Beat thoroughly.

4. Bake in sprayed or paper-lined cupcake pans for 18 to 22 minutes. Yields 18 cupcakes.

Decorations:

1 (12 ounce) container ready-to-
serve vanilla frosting
1 fresh orange
Sugar

1. Spread frosting over top of cupcakes using an icing spatula or back of a spoon.

2. Carefully cut strips of orange peel (do not get any white pith) and roll in a little sugar. Arrange orange strips (zest) on top of cupcakes.

Q. Why did Tommy hit his birthday cake with a hammer?
A. It was a pound cake!

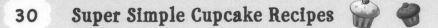

 # Triple Chocolate Birthday Cupcakes

1 (18 ounce) box triple chocolate
    fudge cake mix
⅓ cup canola oil
3 eggs
1 (12 ounce) package swirled
    chocolate and white chocolate
    chips

1. Preheat oven to 350°.

2. Place paper baking cups in 24 muffin cups.
   Combine cake mix, 1¼ cups water, oil and
   eggs in bowl. Beat on low speed for
   30 seconds. Increase speed to medium and
   beat for 2 minutes. Stir in chocolate chips
   and spoon into muffin cups.

3. Bake for 19 to 23 minutes or until toothpick
   inserted in center comes out clean. Cool in
   pan for about 10 minutes. Cool completely
   before frosting. Yields 24 cupcakes.

Decorations:

**1 (16 ounce) container chocolate
    fudge frosting
24 candles**

1. Spread frosting in swirling motions on each cupcake. Place 1 candle on a cupcake.

2. For chocolate lovers who are not celebrating a birthday, set aside about ¾ cup swirled chocolate and white chocolate chips (don't add to batter) and sprinkle 5 to 8 chips on top of frosting – looks great!

In 1939, Nestlé introduced chocolate chips.

Make Your Own Pastry Bag

Make your own pastry bag with a 2-quart plastic bag. Cut small hole in one of the bottom corners. Start with a small hole – you can always make it bigger if you want.

Fill bag half-way with frosting and seal at the top. Slowly squeeze frosting through the small hole and decorate.

You don't have to have special tips unless you want pretty swirls and designs.

How to Use a Pastry Bag or a Plastic Bag to Decorate

A pastry bag is a cone-shaped bag with a small hole for a decorating tip on one end and a larger hole on the other end to fill bag with frosting.

Before adding the frosting, insert tip into bag and through small hole. Screw coupler ring of tip on outside of bag around tip. Make sure it is air-tight with no way for frosting to leak out.

(Special tips are made for pastry bags to create different effects. You can also use plastic bags with the tips.)

Any Day Everyday Cupcakes

White Velvet Cupcakes

1 (18 ounce) box white cake mix
⅓ cup canola oil
1 teaspoon almond extract
3 large egg whites
1 cup white chocolate chips

1. Preheat oven to 350°.

2. Place paper baking cups in 24 muffin cups. Beat cake mix, 1¼ cups water, oil, almond extract and egg whites in bowl on low speed for 30 seconds.

3. Increase speed to medium and beat for 2 minutes. Stir in white chocolate chips. Divide batter among muffin cups.

4. Bake for 19 to 22 minutes or until toothpick inserted in center comes out clean. Cool for 10 minutes before removing from pan. Cool for 30 minutes before frosting. Yields 24 cupcakes.

Decorations:

1 (16 ounce) container ready-to-serve classic white frosting
1 (2 ounce) bottle red or pink sanding sugar or sprinkles

1. Use a pastry bag (or plastic bag with a bottom corner cut off) fitted with a closed star tip number 28 or 30, depending on the size you want.

2. Squeeze bag evenly around cupcake from outside to inside. Scatter colored sanding sugar or sprinkles on top.

December 15th is National Cupcake Day!

Double Butterscotch Cupcakes

2 cups flour
1¼ cups sugar
1 (3.4 ounce) package instant
    butterscotch pudding mix
1 (3.4 ounce) package instant vanilla
    pudding mix
2 teaspoons baking powder
4 eggs, lightly beaten
¾ cup canola oil
1 teaspoon vanilla
1 (12 ounce) package butterscotch
    chips

1. Preheat oven to 350°.

2. Place paper baking cups in 24 muffin cups.
    Combine flour, sugar, both pudding mixes,
    baking powder and ½ teaspoon salt
    in bowl.

3. In separate bowl, combine 1 cup water,
    eggs, oil and vanilla; stir this mixture into

dry ingredients and mix just until moist.
Stir in 1 cup butterscotch chips and
mix well.

4. Spoon batter into muffin cups about
two-thirds full. Bake for 16 to 20 minutes or
until toothpick inserted in center comes out
clean. Cool for 5 minutes before removing
from pan. Cool completely before frosting.
Yields 24 cupcakes.

Decorations:

1 (12 ounce) container ready-to-
    serve buttercream frosting
1 (8 ounce) package toffee bits

1. Use a pastry bag (or plastic bag with a
bottom corner cut off) fitted with a star
tip number 28 or 30, depending on the
size you want. Squeeze bag evenly around
cupcake from outside to inside. Sprinkle
toffee on top.

2. If you wanted a little different twist for the
frosting, coconut-pecan frosting is great on
these cupcakes.

Vanilla-Cinnamon Cupcakes

2½ cups flour
1 (3.4 ounce) package instant French
    vanilla pudding mix
2 teaspoons ground cinnamon
½ teaspoon baking powder
½ teaspoon baking soda
⅓ cup sugar
3 eggs
1 cup buttermilk*
½ cup canola oil
1 teaspoon vanilla
1 cup miniature semi-sweet
    chocolate chips

1. Preheat oven to 350°.

2. Combine flour, pudding mix, cinnamon, baking powder, baking soda, sugar and a little salt in bowl.

3. In separate bowl, combine eggs, buttermilk, oil and vanilla; mix well and add mixture to dry ingredients. Whisk for 1 to 2 minutes and fold in chocolate chips.

4. Place paper baking cups in 18 muffin cups and fill with batter about two-thirds full.

5. Bake for 18 to 21 minutes or until a toothpick inserted in center comes out clean. Cool for about 5 minutes before removing from pan. Allow cupcakes to cool completely before frosting. Yields 18 cupcakes.

Decorations:

1 (12 ounce) container ready-to-serve vanilla frosting
1 teaspoon vanilla
Cinnamon

1. Combine frosting and vanilla. Spread frosting over all cupcakes using pastry bag (or plastic bag with a bottom corner cut off) fitted with large star tip. Sprinkle with cinnamon.

TIP: To make buttermilk, mix 1 cup milk with 1 tablespoon lemon juice or vinegar and let milk stand for about 10 minutes.

Surprise Cupcakes

1 (8 ounce) package cream cheese,
    softened
2 cups sugar, divided
1 egg, slightly beaten
1 cup white chocolate chips
1½ cups flour
1 teaspoon baking soda
⅓ cup canola oil

1. Preheat oven to 350°.

2. Place paper baking cups in 18 muffin cups.
    Combine cream cheese, ½ cup sugar, oil
    and egg in bowl and beat until mixture is
    smooth; stir in white chocolate chips.

3. In separate bowl, combine remaining
    1½ cups sugar, flour, baking soda, oil
    and 1 cup water and mix well, but not
    too vigorously.

4. Fill muffin cups one-third full with batter
    and place 1 heaping tablespoon cream
    cheese mixture over each cupcake. (You
    may need to add a little to each cupcake to
    use up all the cream cheese mixture.)

5. Bake for 20 to 24 minutes or until toothpick inserted in center comes out clean. Cool on wire rack. Remove cupcakes from pan and cool completely before storing. Yields 18 cupcakes.

Decorations:

Powdered sugar
Fresh fruit

1. Frost these cupcakes with a heavy dusting of powdered sugar and top with fresh fruit. Raspberries are great with white chocolate!

Cupcakes are best the day you bake them.

Creamy Butter Cupcakes

1 (18 ounce) box yellow cake mix
½ cup (1 stick) butter, softened
1 egg
1 (8 ounce) package cream cheese,
   softened
1 (16 ounce) box powdered sugar
1 cup chopped nuts

1. Preheat oven to 350°.

2. Place paper baking cups in 16 muffin cups.

3. Mix cake mix, butter and egg with fork until mixture is moist. Fill muffin cups about half full and press down a little.

4. Combine cream cheese, powdered sugar and nuts and beat well. Pour on top of cake mix batter.

5. Bake for about 15 to 20 minutes until toothpick inserted in center comes out clean. Yields 16 cupcakes.

Decorations:

1. These cupcakes are yummy just as they are, but you can choose a frosting or icing from pages 179 to 215. Or top with Spiced Whipped Cream on page 211.

Q. What do they serve at birthday parties in heaven?
A. Angel food cake!
Q. What do they serve in the other place?
A. Devil's food cake!

Blue Moon Cupcakes

1 (18 ounce) box white cake mix
3 eggs
⅓ cup canola oil
1 teaspoon almond extract
1 (12 ounce) package white
    chocolate chips

1. Preheat oven to 350°.

2. Place paper baking cups in 16 muffin cups.

3. Beat cake mix, 1¼ cups water, eggs, oil and almond extract in bowl on low speed for 30 seconds. Increase speed to medium and beat for 2 minutes.

4. Stir in white chocolate chips and mix well. Spoon into muffin cups and bake for 15 to 20 minutes or until toothpick inserted into center comes out clean.

5. Cool for 10 minutes before removing from pan. Cool completely before frosting. Yields 16 cupcakes.

Decorations:

1 (16 ounce) container white
    frosting
1 or 2 drops blue food coloring
24 Party Toppers white candy stars*

1. Place white frosting in small bowl and stir in 1 drop blue food coloring. Add a second drop if you want a deeper color of blue.

2. While stirring in the food coloring, add 1 tablespoon water and mix. (This makes the frosting a little thinner so you can let some of the frosting drip drown the sides in a few places.)

TIP: The Party Topper stars are in craft shops, cake decorating supply store, etc.; they usually come in 6-ounce packages.

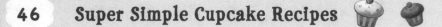

White and Dark Chocolate Cupcakes

1 (18 ounce) box French vanilla
    cake mix
⅓ cup canola oil
3 eggs
1 teaspoon vanilla
1 cup white chocolate chips
    or 1 cup dark chocolate chips
    or ½ cup white chocolate and
      ½ cup dark chocolate chips

1. Preheat oven to 350°.

2. Place paper baking cups in 24 muffin cups.
   Combine cake mix, 1¼ cups water, oil,
   eggs and vanilla in bowl and beat on low
   for 30 seconds.

3. Increase speed to medium and beat for
   2 minutes. Stir in white chocolate chips.
   Spoon evenly into muffin cups.

4. Bake for 18 to 23 minutes or until toothpick inserted in center comes out clean.

5. Cool for 5 minutes before removing from pan. Cool for 30 minutes before frosting. Yields 24 cupcakes.

Decorations:

1 (16 ounce) container ready-to-serve white frosting
24 edible sugar flowers

1. Use a pastry bag (or plastic bag with a bottom corner cut off) fitted with a star tip number 35 or 54, depending on the size you want.

2. Squeeze bag evenly around cupcake from outside to inside.

3. Place edible sugar flower and leaf on top. An advanced class in decorating teaches how to make flowers and leaves.

TIP: Instead of the flowers, you can always use a Hershey® bar and a potato peeler to make some chocolate curls.

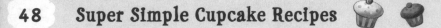

French Vanilla-Chocolate Cupcakes

1 (18 ounce) box French vanilla
    cake mix
⅓ cup canola oil
3 eggs
1 (8 ounce) package milk chocolate
    toffee bits

1. Preheat oven to 350°.

2. Place paper baking cups in 16 muffin cups.
    Combine cake mix, 1¼ cups water, oil
    and eggs in bowl and beat on low for
    30 seconds.

3. Increase speed to medium and beat for
    2 minutes. Stir in chocolate toffee bits and
    mix well. Spoon into muffin cups.

4. Bake for 15 to 20 minutes or until toothpick inserted in center comes out clean. Cool for 5 minutes before removing from pan. Cool completely before frosting. Yields 16 cupcakes.

Decorations:

1 (16 ounce) container milk chocolate frosting
1 (3 ounce) container multi-color sprinkles

1. Place chocolate frosting in medium plastic bag, cut off a bottom corner and squeeze frosting over cupcake in swirling motion. Scatter a few multicolor sprinkles over top of cupcakes.

2. For a change of pace, substitute white frosting and sprinkle with candy Jumbo daisies, hearts, diamonds, stars, etc. in whatever color you like.

White Chocolate Explosion

1 (18 ounce) box white cake mix
3 eggs
⅓ cup canola oil
1 teaspoon almond extract
1½ cups M&M's® chocolate mini bits

1. Preheat oven to 350°.

2. Place paper baking cups in 16 muffin cups.
    Combine cake mix, eggs, oil, almond extract
    and 1¼ cups water in bowl and beat on low
    speed for 30 seconds.

3. Increase speed to medium and beat for
    2 minutes. Stir in M&M's® and spoon into
    muffin cups.

4. Bake for 15 to 20 minutes or until toothpick
    inserted into center comes out clean.
    Cool in pan for about 5 minutes. Cool
    completely before frosting. Yields
    16 cupcakes.

Decorations:

1 (16 ounce) container chocolate
    fudge frosting
1 (4 ounce) tube decorating
    white icing

1. Spread chocolate frosting over cupcakes.
    Use white icing to form "snowflake" over
    chocolate frosting.

2. There are Party Topper candy snowflakes
    and other white items Jumbo Diamonds,
    Jumbo Jimmies, etc. in craft stores.

The only way to have a friend is to be one.
Ralph Waldo Emerson

Granola-Chocolate Chip Cupcakes

1 cup granola cereal
1⅓ cups flour
½ cup sugar
2 teaspoons baking powder
¾ teaspoon baking soda
2 eggs, beaten
1 (8 ounce) carton plain yogurt
⅓ cup canola oil
½ teaspoon vanilla
½ cup chopped pecans
1 cup chocolate chips

1. Preheat oven to 350°.

2. Place paper baking cups in 24 muffin cups. Combine cereal, flour, sugar, baking powder, baking soda and a pinch of salt in large bowl.

3. In smaller bowl, combine eggs, yogurt, oil and vanilla and stir into dry ingredients just until moist. Stir in pecans and chocolate chips.

4. Fill muffin cups three-fourths full with batter and bake for 13 to 15 minutes or until toothpick inserted in center comes out clean.

5. Cool in pan for about 5 minutes. Remove from pan and cool completely before frosting. Yields 12 cupcakes.

Decorations:

1 (16 ounce) ready-to-serve milk chocolate frosting, optional
        or
¾ cup chopped nuts, toasted*

1. These are delicious as is, but if you want a topping one of the above suggestions will be terrific.

*TIP: To toast nuts, spread out on baking sheet and bake at 250° for 10 to 15 minutes. Toasting brings out the flavor in nuts.

Chocolate Chip Cupcakes

1 (18 ounce) box yellow cake mix
3 eggs
⅓ cup canola oil
1 teaspoon vanilla
1 (12 ounce) package chocolate
    chips
1 cup chopped pecans, optional

1. Preheat oven to 350°.

2. Place paper baking cups in 24 muffin cups.
    Combine cake mix, 1¼ cups water, eggs, oil
    and vanilla in bowl.

3. Beat on low speed for 30 seconds, increase
    speed to medium and beat for 2 minutes.
    Fold in chocolate chips and pecans and
    spoon batter into muffin cups.

4. Bake for 19 to 22 minutes or until toothpick
    inserted in center comes out clean. Cool for
    5 to 10 minutes in pan. Remove from pan

and place cupcakes on wire rack to cool completely before frosting. Yields 24 cupcakes.

Decorations:

1. These cupcakes do not really need a frosting, but if you want that "sugar splurge", a chocolate frosting would do well. You could call it Double-Chocolate, Chocolate Chip!

Keep in mind that the smaller the cupcake, the quicker it cooks. The longer it cooks, the drier it will be.

Harvest Pumpkin Cupcakes

1 (15 ounce) can pumpkin
3 eggs, slightly beaten
½ cup oil
1½ teaspoons ground cinnamon
1 teaspoon baking soda
1 (18 ounce) box yellow cake mix
½ cup chopped walnuts

1. Preheat oven to 350°.

2. Place paper baking cups in 24 muffin cups. Combine pumpkin, eggs, oil, cinnamon and baking soda in bowl and mix well.

3. Add cake mix, ¼ cup water and beat for 1 minute on low speed. Increase speed to high and beat for 2 minutes. Fold in walnuts.

4. Fill muffin cups two-thirds full and bake for 19 to 22 minutes or until toothpick inserted in center comes out clean.

5. Cool for 10 minutes in pan; remove from pan and cool completely before frosting. Yields 24 cupcakes.

Decorations:

1 (16 ounce) container ready-to-serve buttercream frosting
1 (2 ounce) bottle yellow, brown and orange sprinkles

1. Spread frosting in swirling motion over cupcakes and top with sprinkles.

2. If you like, use 1 (2 ounce) bottle sugar-cinnamon gems instead of sprinkles. The cinnamon gems really complement the pumpkin in the cupcakes.

Spicy Cupcakes

½ cup shortening
1 cup sugar
2 egg yolks
⅓ cup chopped raisins
⅓ cup chopped walnuts
1 teaspoon baking soda
2½ cups flour
½ teaspoon ground cloves
½ teaspoon ground mace
1½ teaspoons ground cinnamon
¾ cup buttermilk*
1 egg white, stiffly beaten

1. Preheat oven to 350°.

2. Cream shortening, sugar and egg yolks in mixing bowl. Add raisins and walnuts. Dissolve baking soda in 1 tablespoon hot water and add to mixture.

3. Mix and sift flour, ½ teaspoon salt and spices and add alternately with buttermilk to first mixture. Fold in one stiffly beaten egg white.

4. Turn in sprayed or paper-lined muffin cups and bake for 15 to 20 minutes. Yields 18 cupcakes.

Decorations:

Ready-to-serve cream cheese frosting
18 walnut halves

1. Use a pastry bag (or plastic bag with a bottom corner cut off) fitted with a ruffle tip number 86 or 100, depending on the size you want.

2. Squeeze bag evenly around cupcake from outside to inside. If you don't have these tips, try a star tip. Top with walnut halves.

TIP: To make buttermilk, mix 1 cup milk with 1 tablespoon lemon juice or vinegar and let milk stand for about 10 minutes.

Maple-Cream Cupcakes

1½ cups flour
⅓ cup sugar
3 teaspoons baking powder
1 teaspoon ground cinnamon
1 teaspoon ground nutmeg
¼ cup shortening
¾ cup quick-cooking oats
1 egg, beaten
½ cup milk
½ cup maple syrup

1. Preheat oven to 350°.

2. Place paper baking cups in 16 muffin cups.
   Sift flour, sugar, baking powder, ¼ teaspoon
   salt, cinnamon and nutmeg in bowl. Cut
   in shortening until mixture resembles
   coarse crumbs.

3. Stir in oats; add egg, milk and maple syrup;
   stir only until dry ingredients are moist. Fill
   muffin cups one-half full.

4. Bake for 18 to 21 minutes. Let stand in
   pan for about 5 minutes. Cool completely
   before frosting. Yields 16 cupcakes.

Decorations:

1 (12 ounce) container ready-to-
        serve buttercream frosting
2 tablespoons maple syrup
1 tablespoon butter, melted
Ground cinnamon

1. Place buttercream frosting in small bowl,
    stir in maple syrup and melted butter;
    blend well.

2. Use a pastry bag (or plastic bag with a
    bottom corner cut off) fitted with a round
    tip number 10 to 12, depending on the size
    you want. Start in the middle, squeeze bag
    evenly and slowly pull straight up.

3. Sprinkle frosting with cinnamon. Coconut-
    pecan frosting with a sprinkling of finely
    chopped pecans would also be great
    with these.

Creamy Apple Cupcakes

1 (3 ounce) package cream cheese, softened
1 cup sugar
2 eggs
½ cup milk
¼ cup (½ stick) butter, melted
1 tablespoon lemon juice
1 teaspoon vanilla
1½ cups flour
1½ teaspoons baking powder
½ teaspoon baking soda
1 tart apple, peeled, diced
½ cup bran flakes

1. Preheat oven to 350°.

2. Place paper baking cups in 14 muffin cups. Combine cream cheese, sugar, eggs, milk, butter, lemon juice and vanilla in bowl and beat until smooth.

3. In separate bowl, combine flour, baking powder, baking soda and ¼ teaspoon salt and stir into cream cheese mixture just until moist. Fold in diced apples and bran flakes.

4. Spread batter into muffin cups two-thirds full. Bake for 21 to 25 minutes or until toothpick inserted in center comes out clean. Cool in pan for about 5 minutes.

5. Remove to wire rack to cool completely. These cupcakes need to be refrigerated. Yields 14 cupcakes.

Decorations:

1 (12 ounce) container ready-to-serve cream cheese frosting
4 walnuts, shelled, quartered

1. Use a pastry bag (or plastic bag with a bottom corner cut off) fitted with an open star tip number 17 or 21, depending on the size you want. Squeeze bag evenly in four sections to make wings of butterfly. Put a walnut quarter on top to form the body.

TIP: *Dutch Apple-Nut Crumble Topping on page 212 is a great topping to change up this recipe and it's so easy.*

Springtime Apple Cupcakes

1 (19 ounce) box apple streusel
    muffin mix
⅔ cup milk
¼ cup canola oil
1 egg
½ teaspoon ground cinnamon
¾ cup chopped pecans

1. Preheat oven to 400°.

2. Place paper baking cups in 14 muffin cups.

3. Stir muffin mix, milk, oil, egg and cinnamon
    in large bowl just until moist. (Batter will
    be lumpy.)

4. Cut off top of apple filling pouch and
    squeeze apple filling into batter; add
    pecans and stir gently. Fill muffin cups
    about two-thirds full.

5. Sprinkle streusel packet over batter in each muffin cup and bake for 16 to 20 minutes or until golden brown. Cool for at least 5 minutes in pan; cool completely before frosting. Yields 14 cupcakes.

Decorations:

1 (12 ounce) container buttercream frosting

1. Spread buttercream frosting over cupcakes.

TIP: Another "happy" frosting is vanilla "funfetti".

Apples are actually part of the rose family.

Sweet Banana-Strawberry Cupcakes

½ cup (1 stick) butter, softened
½ cup sugar
⅓ cup packed brown sugar
2 large ripe bananas, mashed
2 large eggs
1 teaspoon vanilla
2¼ cups flour
2 teaspoons baking powder
½ teaspoon baking soda
½ cup buttermilk*
½ cup strawberry preserves
1 cup milk chocolate chips

1. Preheat oven to 350°.

2. Place paper baking cups in 18 muffin cups.
   Beat butter, sugar and brown sugar in bowl
   until light and fluffy. Beat in bananas, eggs
   and vanilla.

3. In separate bowl, combine flour, baking
   powder, baking soda and a pinch of salt.

4. Alternately add one-third flour mixture and half of buttermilk to butter mixture and end with flour mixture. Stir in strawberry preserves and chocolate chips.

5. Divide batter evenly among muffin cups and bake for 21 to 25 minutes or until toothpick inserted in center comes out clean. Cool in pan for about 5 minutes. Cool completely before frosting. Yields 18 cupcakes.

Decorations:

1 (16 ounce) container ready-to-serve strawberry frosting
Nonpareils

1. Use a pastry bag (or plastic bag with a bottom corner cut off) fitted with an open star tip number 17 or 21, depending on the size you want. Squeeze bag evenly around cupcake from outside to inside. Scatter nonpareils or sprinkles on top.

TIP: To make buttermilk, mix 1 cup milk with 1 tablespoon lemon juice or vinegar and let milk stand for about 10 minutes.

Banana-Nut Cupcakes

1 (18 ounce) box banana nut cake mix
⅔ cup milk
2 tablespoons canola oil
1 egg

1. Preheat oven to 350°.

2. Place paper baking cups in 12 muffin cups. Combine cake mix, milk, oil and egg in medium bowl. Stir mixture just until it blends well. (Batter will be slightly lumpy.)

3. Divide batter among muffin cups and sprinkle walnuts from cake mix evenly over batter.

4. Bake for about 20 minutes or until golden brown and tops spring back when touched. Cool in pan for 10 minutes; cool completely before frosting. Yields 12 cupcakes.

Decorations:

1 (12 ounce) container ready-to-serve buttercream frosting
1 (2 ounce) bottle pastel sprinkles

1. Use a pastry bag (or plastic bag with a bottom corner cut off) fitted with an open star tip number 17 or 19, depending on the size you want. Squeeze bag evenly around cupcake from outside to inside. Top with sprinkles.

Create a colorful assortment of cupcakes by dividing white frosting into several small bowls and stirring in a drop or two of food coloring in each bowl.

Banana-Chocolate Chip Cupcakes

½ cup (1 stick) butter, softened
⅔ cup sugar
½ cup packed brown sugar
2 eggs
1½ cups (about 3) mashed ripe
     bananas
3 teaspoons vanilla
2 cups flour
3 teaspoons baking soda
1 cup chopped pecans
1 (6 ounce) package milk chocolate
     chips

1. Preheat oven to 350°.

2. Place paper baking cups in 24 muffin cups. Cream butter, sugar and brown sugar in bowl until smooth. Beat in eggs, bananas and vanilla.

3. In separate bowl, combine flour and baking soda and add to creamed mixture just until it blends well. Stir in pecans and chocolate chips and fill muffin cups half full.

4. Bake for 16 to 20 minutes or until a toothpick inserted in center comes out clean. Cool for 5 minutes before removing from pan. Cool completely before frosting. Yields 24 cupcakes.

Decorations:

1 (16 ounce) container ready-to-serve buttercream frosting
1½ cups mini chocolate chips
24 mini chocolate chip cookies, optional

1. Use a pastry bag (or plastic bag with a bottom corner cut off) fitted with an open star tip number 17 or 21, depending on the size you want.

2. Squeeze bag evenly around cupcake from outside to inside, but let the cupcake show.

3. Sprinkle mini chocolate chips over frosting. Place a mini chocolate chip cookie in frosting.

Blueberry-Spice Cupcakes

¾ cup sugar
½ cup (1 stick) butter, softened
1¾ cups plus 1 tablespoon flour
2½ teaspoons baking powder
¾ teaspoon ground cinnamon
¼ teaspoon ground nutmeg
1 egg, lightly beaten
¾ cup milk
1½ cups fresh blueberries

1. Preheat oven to 350°.

2. Place paper baking cups in 12 muffin cups.
   Cream sugar and butter. In separate bowl,
   combine flour, baking powder, cinnamon,
   nutmeg and ¼ teaspoon salt.

3. Add egg and milk to sugar-butter mixture
   and stir in dry ingredients just until moist.
   Gently fold in blueberries.

4. Spoon batter into muffin cups about
   two-thirds full. Bake for 17 to 21 minutes

or until toothpick inserted in center comes out clean. Cool for 5 minutes before removing from pan. Let cupcakes completely cool before frosting. Yields 12 cupcakes.

Decorations:

1 (12 ounce) container ready-to-serve white frosting
White fondant
Edible flowers or chocolate bar, optional

1. Spread a thin coat of frosting over top of cupcake to keep crumbs out of fondant. Lay white fondant on top and trim around liner.

2. Top with edible sugar flowers or paint your own with tube of decorating gel.

3. If you don't have any decoration for the cupcake, put some blueberries on top.

TIP: *For a quick cupcake decoration, hold a chocolate bar on its side and use a potato peeler to make chocolate curls.*

Cherry-Honey Cupcakes

1½ cups quick-cooking oats
1 cup flour
⅓ cup packed brown sugar
3 teaspoons baking powder
1 egg
⅔ cup milk
⅓ cup canola oil
⅓ cup honey
18 to 24 fresh sweet cherries,
   coarsely chopped

1. Preheat oven to 350°.

2. Place paper baking cups in 18 muffin cups. Combine oats, flour, brown sugar, baking powder and a pinch of salt in large bowl.

3. In separate bowl, combine egg, milk, oil and honey and stir into dry ingredients just until moist. Stir in cherries and pour into muffin cups, about two-thirds full.

4. Bake for 16 to 18 minutes or until toothpick inserted in center comes out clean.

5. Cool in pan for about 5 minutes. Cool completely before frosting. Yields 18 cupcakes.

Decorations:

1 (12 ounce) container vanilla frosting
18 maraschino cherries

1. Use a pastry bag (or plastic bag with a bottom corner cut off) fitted with an open star tip number 17 or 21 or closed star tip number 30 or 35

2. Squeeze bag evenly around cupcake from outside to inside, but let some of the cupcake show. Top with cherry.

Carrot Cake Cupcakes

1 (18 ounce) box carrot cake mix
3 eggs
½ cup canola oil
1 (8 ounce) can crushed pineapple
       with juice
¾ cup chopped pecans

1. Preheat oven to 350°.

2. Place paper baking cups in 24 muffin cups.
   Mix cake mix, eggs, oil, pineapple and
   ½ cup water in bowl and beat on low
   speed for 1 minute.

3. Increase speed to medium and beat for
   2 minutes. Fold in pecans and spoon into
   muffin cups.

4. Bake for 19 to 23 minutes or until toothpick
   inserted in center comes out clean. Cool in
   pan for 5 minutes. Remove cupcakes from
   pan and cool completely before frosting.
   Yields 24 cupcakes.

Decorations:

1 (16 ounce) container ready-to-
 serve cream cheese frosting
Food coloring
24 sugar or fondant carrots,
 optional
Powdered sugar, optional
Pecan pieces, optional

1. Use a pastry bag (or plastic bag with a bottom corner cut off) fitted with a round tip number 5. It's good for thin lines, writing and dots. Tips 2, 3, 4 have smaller holes and will make finer lines, but they may be too small for some icings.

2. Add food coloring to remaining frosting as needed. Make a carrot with a large round tip number 2A or 1A. The carrot stem needs an open star tip about number 15.

3. The easiest topping for these cupcakes is to sprinkle powdered sugar and pecan pieces over the top.

Quick 7UP Cupcakes

1 (18 ounce) box lemon cake mix
¾ cup oil
1 (3.4 ounce) box lemon pudding mix
4 eggs
1 (10 ounce) bottle 7UP®

1. Preheat oven to 350°.

2. Place paper baking cups in 18 muffin cups.

3. Combine all ingredients and beat on low speed for 30 seconds. Increase speed to medium and beat for 2 minutes.

4. Pour batter into muffin cups, filling about three-fourths full.

5. Bake for about 15 to 20 minutes until toothpick inserted in center comes out clean. Cool completely before frosting. Yields 18 cupcakes.

Decorations:

1 (6 ounce) can crushed pineapple,
    drained
1½ cups sugar
1 cup flaked coconut
½ cup (1 stick) butter, softened

1. Mix all ingredients and top cupcakes.

More statistical studies are finding that family meals play a significant role in childhood development. Children who eat with their families four or more nights per week are healthier, make better grades in school, score higher on aptitude tests and are less likely to have problems with drugs.

Fresh Lemon Cupcakes

1 (18 ounce) box lemon cake mix
⅓ cup canola oil
3 eggs
1 (8 ounce) can crushed pineapple,
    drained

1. Preheat oven to 350°.

2. Place paper baking cups in 24 muffin cups.
   Combine cake mix, 1¼ cups water, oil and
   eggs in bowl and beat on low speed for
   30 seconds. Increase mixer speed to
   medium and beat for 2 minutes. Stir in
   pineapple and mix well.

3. Spoon into muffin cups and bake for
   18 to 22 minutes or until toothpick inserted
   in center comes out clean. Cool in pan for
   about 5 minutes. Cool completely before
   frosting. Yields 24 cupcakes.

Decorations:

1 (16 ounce) container ready-to-serve lemon frosting
2 - 3 lemons, thinly sliced

1. Use a pastry bag (or plastic bag with a bottom corner cut off) fitted with a closed star tip number 30 or 31, depending on the size you want.

2. Drop individual flowers over cupcakes; top with thin half slice of lemon.

Using an ice cream scoop that holds about ¼ to ⊠ cup of cupcake batter makes filling cupcake tins much faster. Tins should be filled about three-quarters full.

Sweet Orange Cupcakes

½ cup (1 stick) unsalted butter,
    softened
1¼ cups sugar
2 large eggs
1 (8 ounce) carton plain yogurt
2 cups flour
1 teaspoon baking soda
½ cup chopped pecans
½ cup orange marmalade
1 teaspoon orange extract

1. Preheat oven to 350°.

2. Cream butter and sugar in bowl. Beat in eggs and yogurt for 1 minute. Add flour and baking soda and stir into creamed mixture; stir just until mixture is moist. Fold in pecans, orange marmalade and orange extract.

3. Place paper baking cups in 18 muffin cups and fill muffin cups three-fourths full. Bake for 18 to 21 minutes or until toothpick inserted in center comes out clean.

4. Cool in pan for about 5 minutes. Remove from pan and cool completely before frosting. Yields 18 cupcakes.

Decorations:

**1 (16 ounce) container ready-to-
     serve cream cheese frosting
Orange sanding sugar
Fresh orange slices**

1. Use a pastry bag (or plastic bag with a bottom corner cut off) fitted with a round tip between number 10 or 12, depending on the size you want. Start on the outside, slowly squeeze and pull straight up when finished.

2. Top with sanding sugar and garnish with fresh orange slices.

3. If you want a flavored orange icing, stir ½ cup orange marmalade or 1 tablespoon thawed orange juice concentrate into frosting.

Little Bit of Lime Cupcakes

1 (18 ounce) box yellow cake mix
⅓ cup canola oil
3 eggs
¼ cup sugar
1 tablespoon lime juice
1 teaspoon finely grated lime peel

1. Preheat oven to 350°.

2. Place paper baking cups in 16 muffin cups.
   Combine cake mix, 1¼ cups water, oil, eggs,
   sugar, lime juice and lime peel in bowl.

3. Beat on low speed for 30 seconds; increase
   speed to medium and beat for 2 minutes.
   Spoon into muffin cups.

4. Bake for 15 to 20 minutes or until toothpick
   inserted in center comes out clean. Cool
   for 10 minutes before removing from pan.
   Cool completely before frosting. Yields
   16 cupcakes.

Decorations:

3 limes
1 (16 ounce) container classic
    white frosting

1. Cut limes into 24 very thin slices.

2. Spread each cupcake with white frosting
    and stand 1 slice of lime up in the frosting.

Cupcakes are called "fairy cakes" in England because they were once made in teacups. Small, delicate cakes baked in teacups seemed exactly like what fairies would serve at parties.

Raspberry-Filled Lemon Cupcakes

2 cups flour
2½ teaspoons baking powder
¼ teaspoon baking soda
¾ cup (1½ sticks) unsalted butter,
    softened
1¼ cups sugar
1 egg plus 3 egg yolks
1 tablespoon lemon juice, plus enough
    milk to equal ¾ cup
1 tablespoon grated lemon peel
½ cup seedless raspberry jam

1. Preheat oven to 350°.

2. Place paper baking cups in 16 muffin cups.
   Sift flour, baking powder, baking soda and
   ¼ teaspoon salt in bowl.

3. In separate bowl, beat butter and sugar
   until mixture lightens. Beat in egg and
   egg yolks and mix well. Add flour mixture
   alternating with lemon juice-milk mixture,
   beginning and ending with flour. Stir in
   lemon peel.

4. Spoon heaping ¼ cup batter into each liner and bake for 20 to 23 minutes or until toothpick inserted in center comes out clean. Remove from pan and cool completely on rack before frosting.

5. Poke a hole in center of each cupcake with handle of wooden spoon. Go almost to the bottom while cupcakes are still hot.

6. Place raspberry jam in plastic bag and snip off a small corner. Dip corner of bag into hole and pipe about 1½ teaspoons jam into center of each cupcake. Yields 16 cupcakes.

Decorations:

1 (12 ounce) container ready-to-serve white frosting
1 pint fresh raspberries

1. Spread frosting over top of cupcakes using an icing spatula or back of spoon. Top with fresh raspberries. Lemon icing is also amazing!

Raspberry-Cream Cupcakes

1 (18 ounce) box white cake mix
1 (8 ounce) carton sour cream
½ cup canola oil
2 eggs, slightly beaten
¼ cup raspberry preserves
1 (3 ounce) package cream cheese

1. Preheat oven to 350°.

2. In large bowl, mix cake mix, sour cream, oil, ½ cup water and eggs with spoon. Mix until they blend well. Batter will be thick.

3. Place paper baking cups into 16 muffin cups and divide batter evenly among muffin cups.

4. In small bowl, stir raspberry preserves until fairly smooth. Cut cream cheese into 24 pieces and place 1 piece cream cheese on top of batter in each muffin cup and gently press down.

5. Place about ½ teaspoon preserves over cream cheese and bake for 20 to 24 minutes. Cool completely.

Decorations:

1 (16 ounce) container cream cheese frosting
Sliced fresh raspberries

1. Frost with cream cheese frosting and place 1 sliced raspberry on top.

If you want a smooth surface on top of your cupcakes, frost them as usual, then dip a knife in hot water and gently smooth the frosting.

Tempting Berry Cupcakes

¾ cup fresh blueberries
¾ cup coarsely chopped fresh
    strawberries
1 cup sugar, divided
1 (8 ounce) package cream cheese,
    softened
2 eggs
1 teaspoon vanilla
1¼ cups flour
1 teaspoon baking soda

1. Preheat oven to 350°.

2. Place paper baking cups in 12 muffin cups.
   Combine blueberries, strawberries and
   ¼ cup sugar in bowl and set aside.

3. In separate bowl, beat cream cheese and
   remaining sugar until mixture is smooth.
   Add eggs one at a time and beat well after
   each addition; stir in vanilla.

4. Combine flour, baking soda and pinch of
   salt in bowl and stir into creamed mixture.

Fold in berries and fill muffin cups two-thirds full.

5. Bake for 18 to 21 minutes or until toothpick inserted in center comes out clean. Cool for about 5 minutes before removing from pan.

6. Cool completely on wire rack before frosting. These cupcakes need to be refrigerated. Yields 12 cupcakes.

Decorations:

1 (12 ounce) container ready-to-serve cream cheese frosting
1 pint fresh strawberries, sliced to stem

1. Use a pastry bag (or plastic bag with a bottom corner cut off) fitted with an open star tip number 17 or 21 to place a thick layer of cream cheese frosting over cupcakes. Place strawberries on top of frosting.

TIP: *Using frozen berries for cupcakes instead of fresh berries makes cupcakes heavier because they have much more liquid than fresh berries.*

Creamy Strawberry Cupcakes

1 (18 ounce) box super-moist yellow
    cake mix
1 (8 ounce) carton sour cream
½ cup canola oil
2 eggs
¼ cup strawberry preserves at room
    temperature
1 (3 ounce) package cream cheese,
    cut into 24 pieces

1. Preheat oven to 350°.

2. Place paper baking cups in 24 muffin cups.
   Combine cake mix, sour cream, oil, ½ cup
   water and eggs in large bowl with spoon
   until they blend well. (Batter will be thick.)
   Divide batter evenly among muffin cups.

3. In separate bowl, stir strawberry preserves
   until smooth. Place 1 piece cream cheese
   on top of batter in each cupcake and press

down slightly. Place ¼ teaspoon preserves over cream cheese.

4. Bake for 18 to 23 minutes or until tops are golden brown and toothpick inserted in center comes out clean. Cool for 10 minutes before removing from pan. Cool completely before frosting. These cupcakes need to be refrigerated. Yields 24 cupcakes.

Decorations:

1 (16 ounce) container ready-to-serve strawberry frosting
1 (3 ounce) bottle nonpareils or sprinkles

1. Use a pastry bag (or plastic bag with a bottom corner cut off) fitted with an open star tip number 16 or 18, depending on the size you want.

2. Squeeze bag evenly around cupcake from outside to inside, but let some of the cupcake show. Drop sprinkles or nonpareils on top.

Strawberry Delight

1 (18 ounce) box strawberry
 cake mix
3 eggs
⅛ cup canola oil
1 (6 ounce) package white
 chocolate chips

1. Preheat oven to 350°.

2. Place paper baking cups in 24 muffin cups. Combine cake mix, eggs, oil and 1¼ cups water in bowl and beat on low speed for about 30 seconds.

3. Increase speed to medium and beat for 2 minutes. Stir in white chocolate chips and spoon about ¼ cup batter into each muffin cup.

4. Bake for 19 to 23 minutes or until toothpick inserted in center comes out clean. Cool in pan for 5 to 10 minutes. Cool completely before frosting. Yields 24 cupcakes.

Decorations:

1 (16 ounce) container ready-to-
    serve strawberry frosting
1 (2 ounce) bottle multi-colored
    sprinkles

1. Use a pastry bag (or plastic bag with a
   bottom corner cut off) fitted with an open
   star tip number 21. Squeeze bag evenly
   around cupcake from outside to inside. Top
   with multi-colored sprinkles.

TIP: If you can't find the right color frosting for
      your cupcakes, don't hesitate to use food
      coloring. Just remember, a little can be a lot
      of color.

Poppy Seed-Strawberry Cupcakes

2 cups flour
¾ cup sugar
1 tablespoon baking powder
1 tablespoon poppy seeds
½ teaspoon ground cinnamon
1 egg
¾ cup milk
¼ cup (½ stick) unsalted butter, melted
½ cup strawberry preserves

1. Preheat oven to 350°.

2. Place paper baking cups in 16 muffin cups. Combine flour, sugar, baking powder, poppy seeds and cinnamon in bowl.

3. In separate bowl, beat egg, milk and butter and stir into dry ingredients just until moist. Fold in strawberry preserves and mix well. Fill muffin cups with batter two-thirds full.

4. Bake for 19 to 23 minutes or until toothpick inserted in center comes out clean and cupcakes are golden brown.

5. Cool for at least 5 minutes before removing from pan. Cool completely before frosting. Yields 16 cupcakes.

Decorations:

1 (12 ounce) container ready-to-serve vanilla frosting
1 pint fresh strawberries, halved

1. Spread frosting over cupcakes with icing spatula or back of spoon. Top with strawberry half.

Fruit and Nutty Cupcakes

1 (18 ounce) box moist yellow
    cake mix
⅓ cup canola oil
3 eggs
1 (15 ounce) can fruit cocktail,
    well drained
⅔ cup chopped pecans

1. Preheat oven to 350°.

2. Place paper baking cups in 16 muffin cups.
    Beat cake mix, 1 cup water, oil and eggs in
    large bowl on low speed for 30 seconds.
    Increase speed to medium and beat for
    2 minutes.

3. Fold in fruit cocktail and pecans and mix
    well. Divide batter evenly among muffin
    cups. filling each about three-fourths full.

4. Bake for 15 to 20 minutes or until toothpick inserted in center comes out clean. Cool in pan for 10 minutes. Cool completely before frosting. Yields 16 cupcakes.

Decorations:

1 (16 ounce) container buttercream frosting
1 (2 ounce) bottle rainbow nonpareils
24 fresh strawberries

1. Spread frosting over cupcakes and sprinkle with lots of rainbow nonpareils. Place strawberry on top of each cupcake.

2. You can also top with sugar Party Toppers, like colorful flowers, stars, diamonds, dolls, baseballs, etc.

Fun-Colored Cupcakes

1 (18 ounce) box French vanilla
    cake mix
⅓ cup canola oil
3 eggs
1 (7 ounce) package Tropical Trio® *

1. Preheat oven to 350°.

2. Place paper baking cups in 16 muffin cups.
   Combine cake mix, 1¼ cups water, oil and
   eggs in bowl and beat on low speed for
   30 seconds.

3. Increase speed to medium and beat for
   2 minutes. Stir in tropical fruit and spoon
   into muffin cups.

4. Bake for 15 to 20 minutes or until toothpick
   inserted in center comes out clean. Cool in
   pan 5 to 10 minutes. Remove from pan
   and cool completely before frosting. Yields
   16 cupcakes.

Decorations:

1 (16 ounce) container classic
      white frosting
1 (4 ounce) bottle jumbo nonpareils
Red maraschino cherries without
      stems

1. Spread frosting on cupcakes and sprinkle jumbo nonpareils over frosting. Top each cupcake with 1 cherry.

2. Party Toppers like candy party hats, hearts, flowers, stars and many others could be used instead cherries.

TIP: Tropical Trio® is dried pineapple, papaya and mangoes and is located in the canned fruit section of the grocery store.

Zucchini Cupcakes

These are not too sweet – just right for a quick, healthy lunch box or snack treat.

1½ cups self-rising flour
1 teaspoon baking soda
1½ teaspoons pumpkin pie spice
3 egg whites or ¾ cup egg
　　　substitute
¾ cup packed brown sugar
½ cup canola oil
2 cups peeled, grated zucchini

1. Preheat oven to 350°.

2. Combine flour, baking soda and pumpkin pie spice in small bowl.

3. Beat eggs, brown sugar and oil in mixing bowl for about 3 minutes. Add zucchini and stir until they blend well. Add flour mixture and stir until ingredients combine thoroughly.

4. Fill paper-lined muffin cups three-fourths full and bake for 20 to 25 minutes. Cool pan on wire rack for 5 minutes; let cupcakes cool completely before frosting. Yields 12 cupcakes.

Decorations:

Cream cheese frosting, optional
1½ cups walnut pieces, optional

1. These are delicious without a frosting, but if you want a frosting, cream cheese is delicious with these cupcakes. Frost each cupcake and top with walnut pieces.

When you go on a diet, are you a poor loser?

Brunch-Time Cupcakes

2½ cups flour
1½ cups sugar
2 teaspoons ground cinnamon
2 teaspoons baking soda
3 eggs, lightly beaten
¾ cup applesauce
½ cup canola oil
1 teaspoon vanilla
1½ cups dried cranberries or
    Craisins®
1 tart apple, peeled, grated
1 (8 ounce) can crushed pineapple,
    drained
½ cup flaked coconut
¾ cup chopped pecans

1. Preheat oven to 350°.

2. Place paper baking cups in 24 muffin cups.
   Combine flour, sugar, cinnamon, baking
   soda and ½ teaspoon salt in bowl.

3. In separate bowl, combine eggs, applesauce, oil and vanilla.

4. Stir mixture into dry ingredients just until moist. (Batter will be thick.) Stir in cranberries, apple, pineapple, coconut and pecans.

5. Spoon batter into muffin cups about two-thirds full and bake for 21 to 24 minutes or until toothpick inserted in center comes out clean. Cool in pan for about 5 minutes and cool completely before storing. Yields 24 cupcakes.

Decorations:

These cupcakes are so moist and filled with fruit goodies that they really don't need frosting.

Tropical Coconut Cupcakes

1 (3 ounce) package cream cheese, softened
1⅓ cups sugar
1 teaspoon vanilla
½ teaspoon almond extract
1 egg
2 cups flour
1 teaspoon baking soda
¼ cup sour cream
1 (15 ounce) can crushed pineapple, drained
⅓ cup chopped, slivered almonds
½ cup flaked coconut

1. Preheat oven to 350°.

2. Place paper baking cups in 18 muffin cups. Beat cream cheese, sugar, vanilla and almond extract in bowl until smooth and creamy. Stir in egg and mix well.

3. In separate bowl, combine flour and baking soda and add to creamed mixture

alternately with sour cream, just until moist. Fold in pineapple, almonds and coconut.

4. Fill muffin cups three-fourths full. Bake for 24 to 26 minutes or until toothpick inserted in center comes out clean.

5. Cool in pan for about 10 minutes. Cool completely before frosting. These cupcakes need to be refrigerated. Yields 18 cupcakes.

Decorations:

White frosting
Yellow food coloring
Powdered sugar

1. Mix a few drops of food coloring with frosting. Use a pastry bag (or plastic bag with a bottom corner cut off) fitted with an open star tip number 30 or 54. Squeeze bag evenly around cupcake from outside to inside.

2. Pop in oven broiler for a few seconds until the top is a little brown. Dust with powdered sugar.

Coconut Delight Cupcakes

1 cup flour
2 teaspoons baking powder
¾ cup butter-flavored shortening
½ cup (1 stick) butter, softened
1¼ cups sugar
4 egg whites
¾ cup half-and-half cream
1 teaspoon coconut extract
1 cup flaked coconut

1. Preheat oven to 350°.

2. Place paper baking cups in 14 muffin cups. Combine flour, baking powder and ½ teaspoon salt in bowl.

3. In separate bowl, beat shortening, butter and sugar until creamy. Add egg whites and beat until very light and foamy, about 3 minutes.

4. Add flour mixture, alternating with half-and-half cream, beginning and ending with flour mixture. Stir in coconut extract and

coconut. Spoon scant ⅓ cup batter into each cupcake liner.

5. Bake for 24 to 27 minutes or until toothpick inserted in center comes out clean. Remove from pan and cool completely before frosting. Yields 14 cupcakes.

Decorations:

1 (16 ounce) container ready-to-serve buttercream frosting
Yellow food coloring
Edible sugar flowers, optional

1. Place buttercream in bowl. Add food coloring until frosting reaches desired color. Use a pastry bag (or plastic bag with a bottom corner cut off) fitted with closed star tip number 30. Squeeze bag evenly around cupcake from outside to inside.

2. Place flower on top. If you don't have flowers handy, sprinkle finely grated lemon peel over top.

Chocolate-Strawberry Cupcakes

1 (18 ounce) box milk chocolate
    cake mix
⅓ cup canola oil
3 eggs
1 teaspoon almond extract
1 cup white chocolate chips

1. Preheat oven to 350°.

2. Place paper baking cups in 24 muffin cups.
   Combine cake mix, 1¼ cups water, oil, eggs
   and almond extract in bowl.

3. Beat on low speed for 30 seconds; increase
   speed to medium and beat for 2 minutes.
   Stir in white chocolate chips and spoon into
   muffin cups.

4. Bake for 18 to 22 minutes or until toothpick
   inserted in center comes out clean. Cool for
   10 minutes in pan; then let cool completely
   before frosting. Yields 24 cupcakes.

Decorations:

**1 (16 ounce) container ready-to-
serve strawberry frosting**
**1 (3 ounce) container chocolate
jimmies or sprinkles**

1. Use a pastry bag (or plastic bag with a
bottom corner cut off) fitted with an open
star tip number 21. Squeeze bag evenly
around cupcake from outside to inside. Top
with sprinkles.

2. For a special touch, dip one whole
strawberry with stem in melted chocolate
about half-way to stem and place on top
of cupcakes.

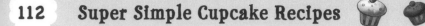

Cherry-Chocolate Cupcakes

1 (18 ounce) box devil's food
   chocolate cake mix
3 large eggs
⅓ cup canola oil
1 teaspoon almond extract
1 (6 ounce) bottle maraschino
   cherries, drained, chopped
1 cup white chocolate chips

1. Preheat oven to 350°.

2. Place paper baking cups in 24 muffin cups.
   Combine cake mix, eggs, oil, almond extract
   and 1¼ cups water in bowl and beat on low
   speed for about 30 seconds. Increase speed
   to medium and beat mixture for 2 minutes.

3. Stir in cherries and white chocolate chips
   and mix well, but gently.

4. Pour into muffin cups and bake for 19 to 23 minutes or until toothpick inserted in center comes out clean. Cool on wire rack for 5 to 10 minutes; cool completely before frosting. Yields 24 cupcakes.

Decorations:

1 (16 ounce) container ready-to-serve cherry frosting
1 (6 ounce) bottle maraschino cherries with stems

1. Spread cherry frosting over cupcakes using knife in swirling motion and top with 1 cherry with stem.

Triple Chocolate Cupcake Cones

1 (18 ounce) box triple chocolate
    fudge cake mix
½ cup canola oil
2 eggs
1 cup chocolate chips
1 (24 count) box flat-bottomed ice
    cream cones

1. Preheat oven to 350°.

2. Combine cake mix, 1¼ cups water, oil
   and eggs in bowl. Beat on low speed for
   30 seconds.

3. Increase speed to medium and beat for
   2 minutes. Stir in chocolate chips and spoon
   into cones within ½ inch of top. Place in
   muffin pan and place crumpled pieces of foil
   where needed to stabilize each cone.

4. Bake for 19 to 23 minutes or until toothpick
   inserted in center comes out clean. Cool

completely before frosting. Yields
24 cupcake cones.

Decorations:

**1 (12 ounce) container ready-to-
serve white frosting
1 (2 ounce) jar chocolate sprinkles**

1. Use a pastry bag (or plastic bag with a
bottom corner cut off) fitted with an open
star tip or even a round tip. Squeeze bag
evenly around cupcake from outside to
inside. Top with chocolate sprinkles.

*Friends are the chocolate chips in the
cookie of life.* Unknown

Chocolate Cupcakes Topped with White Chocolate and Brickle Bits

1 (18 ounce) box devil's food cake mix
3 eggs
⅓ cup canola oil
1 cup chocolate chips

1. Preheat oven to 350°.

2. Place paper baking cups in 24 muffin cups.
   Combine cake mix, 1¼ cups water, eggs
   and oil in bowl and beat on low speed for
   30 seconds.

3. Increase speed to medium and beat for
   2 minutes. Stir in chocolate chips and spoon
   batter into muffin cups.

4. Bake for 21 to 25 minutes or until toothpick
   inserted in center comes out clean. Cool
   for 10 minutes before removing from pan.
   Cool completely before frosting. Yields
   24 cupcakes.

Decorations:

1 (16 ounce) container ready-to-
serve creamy chocolate frosting
1 cup white chocolate chips
1 cup brickle bits

1. Microwave white chocolate chips in microwave-safe bowl on MEDIUM for about 2½ minutes and stir after 1 or 2 minutes. Stir until smooth and cool for 5 minutes. Stir in frosting until mixture blends well.

2. Immediately frost cupcakes. Use a pastry bag (or plastic bag with a bottom corner cut off) fitted with an open star tip number 17 or 21. Squeeze bag evenly around cupcake from outside to inside.

3. These cupcakes are extra pretty sprinkled with white chocolate shavings and brickle bits on top.

White Truffle-Chocolate Cupcakes

1 (18 ounce) box chocolate cake mix
3 large eggs
⅓ cup canola oil
1 teaspoon almond extract
⅓ cup flaked coconut
1 (12 ounce) package white
    chocolate chips

1. Preheat oven to 350°.

2. Place paper baking cups in 24 muffin cups.
   Combine cake mix, eggs, oil, almond extract
   and 1¼ cups water and beat on low speed
   for 30 seconds.

3. Increase speed to medium and beat for
   2 minutes. Stir in coconut and white
   chocolate chips.

4. Pour into muffin cups and bake for 19 to
   23 minutes. Cool in pan for about 5 minutes.
   Cool completely before frosting. Yields
   24 cupcakes.

Decorations:

1 (16 ounce) container ready-to-
  serve fluffy white frosting
Food coloring, optional
1½ cups sweetened flaked coconut
1 (10 ounce) bar dark chocolate bar,
  shaved, optional
1 (10 ounce) bar white chocolate bar,
  shaved, optional

1. Use a pastry bag (or plastic bag with a
    bottom corner cut off) fitted with an open
    star tip number 17 or 21.

2. Squeeze bag evenly around cupcake from
    outside to inside. Sprinkle coconut on top
    and sides. Another idea is to sprinkle with
    chocolate shavings,

TIP: To dye coconut, place a few drops of food
      color in small container and swirl it against
      the sides. Add coconut and mix well or cover
      container with lid and shake.

TIP: Hold chocolate bar on its side and use potato
      peeler to make chocolate curls and shavings.

Cupcake Sundaes

1 (18 ounce) box milk chocolate
    cake mix
⅓ cup canola oil
3 eggs

1. Preheat oven to 350°.

2. Place paper baking cups in 24 muffin cups.
    Combine cake mix, 1¼ cup water, oil and
    eggs in bowl.

3. Beat on low speed for 30 seconds; increase
    speed to medium and beat for 2 minutes.
    Spoon into muffin cups.

4. Bake for 19 to 22 minutes or until toothpick
    inserted in center comes out clean. Cool
    for 5 minutes before removing from pan.
    Cool completely before frosting. Yields
    24 cupcakes.

Decorations:

½ cup vegetable oil
1 tablespoon egg white
2 tablespoons milk
3 cups powdered sugar, sifted
Chocolate syrup
1 (6 ounce) jar maraschino cherries
    with stems

1. Lightly beat vegetable oil, egg white and milk in large bowl. Add half powdered sugar and beat. Add remaining powdered sugar and beat on high for several minutes.

2. Use ice cream scoop to put frosting on cupcake. Drizzle chocolate syrup over cupcake and top with cherry.

Chocolate-Filled Cupcakes

1 (18 ounce) box devil's food cake mix
1⅓ cups buttermilk*
4 eggs, divided
⅓ cup canola oil
1 cup mini semi-sweet chocolate
    chips, divided
1 (8 ounce) package cream cheese,
    softened
½ cup sugar

1. Preheat oven to 350°.

2. Combine cake mix, buttermilk, 3 eggs and
    oil in large bowl. Beat on low speed to
    blend, then beat on medium for 2 minutes.
    Stir ½ cup chocolate chips into batter.

3. In separate bowl, beat cream cheese, sugar
    and remaining egg until mixture is smooth.
    Melt remaining chocolate chips in saucepan
    and add to cream cheese mixture. Beat
    mixture until it blends well.

4. Prepare 24 muffin cups by either spraying and flouring or using paper baking liners. Fill each muffin cup half full with batter.

5. Drop 1 tablespoon chocolate-cream cheese mixture in center and spoon remaining batter evenly over filling. Bake for 25 minutes or until toothpick inserted in center comes out clean. Yields 24 cupcakes.

TIP: To make buttermilk, mix 1 cup milk with 1 tablespoon lemon juice or vinegar and let milk stand for about 10 minutes.

It is best to add 1 teaspoon butter to chocolate when melting it because this will give it a better consistency.

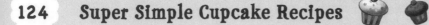
Creme-Filled Chocolate Cupcakes

1 (18 ounce) box double chocolate
    cake mix
½ cup canola oil
1 egg

1. Preheat oven to 350°.

2. Place paper baking cups in 24 muffin cups.
    Stir cake mix, 1 cup water, oil and egg in
    medium bowl just until they blend and
    divide batter among muffin cups.

3. Bake for 18 to 22 minutes. Cool in pan
    for 10 minutes, remove from pan and cool
    completely. Yields 24 cupcakes.

Decorations:

1 (16 ounce) container ready-to-
     serve vanilla frosting
1 cup marshmallow creme
Powdered sugar, optional
Fresh fruit, optional

1. Combine vanilla frosting and marshmallow creme in bowl; mix well.

2. Cut tops off cupcakes.

3. Use a pastry bag (or plastic bag with a bottom corner cut off) fitted with an open star tip number 17 or 21. Squeeze bag evenly around bottom part of cupcake from outside to inside.

4. Replace top of cupcake, sprinkle with powdered sugar and garnish with fresh fruit.

Chocolate-Peanut Butter Cupcakes

1¾ cups flour
1 tablespoon cocoa
2 teaspoons baking powder
¾ cup peanut butter
½ cup (1 stick) butter, softened
1½ cups sugar
2 eggs
¾ cup milk
1 teaspoon vanilla

1. Preheat oven to 350°.

2. Place paper baking cups in 20 muffin cups.
   Whisk flour, cocoa and baking powder in
   medium bowl.

3. In separate bowl, beat peanut butter and
   butter until smooth. Add sugar gradually
   and beat thoroughly. Add eggs, one at
   a time, beating well after each addition,
   about 2 minutes.

4. Add flour mixture, alternating with milk,
   beginning and ending with flour mixture.

Stir in vanilla. Divide batter equally among muffin cups.

5. Bake for 24 to 26 minutes or until toothpick inserted in center comes out clean. Remove from pan and cool completely on wire rack. Yields 20 cupcakes.

Decorations:

1 (16 ounce) container ready-to-serve milk chocolate frosting
½ cup peanut butter
Mini chocolate candies or sprinkles
Miniature jelly beans or equivalent

1. Combine milk chocolate frosting and peanut butter in bowl and mix well.

2. Use a pastry bag (or plastic bag with a bottom corner cut off) fitted with an open star tip number 21 or 22. Leave some cupcake showing and squeeze bag evenly around cupcake from outside to inside. Decorate with sprinkles, jelly beans, etc.

Peanutty Chocolate Cupcakes

1 (18 ounce) box chocolate fudge
    cake mix
⅓ cup canola oil
3 eggs
1 teaspoon almond extract
1 (6 ounce) package white chocolate
    chips

1. Preheat oven to 350°.

2. Place paper baking cups in 16 muffin cups.
   Combine cake mix, 1¼ cups water, oil, eggs
   and almond extract in bowl.

3. Beat on low speed for 30 seconds; increase
   speed and beat for 2 minutes. Stir in white
   chocolate chips. Spoon into muffin cups.

4. Bake for 15 to 20 minutes or until toothpick inserted in center comes out clean. Cool for 5 minutes in pan. Cool completely before frosting. Yields 16 cupcakes.

Decorations:

1 (16 ounce) container chocolate fudge frosting
1 cup finely chopped peanuts

1. Spread chocolate fudge frosting on each cupcake and sprinkle with chopped peanuts.

2. If peanuts don't impress you, use chopped pecans, chopped walnuts or toasted, slivered almonds.

Chocolate Fudge Cupcakes

1 (18 ounce) box butter-fudge
    cake mix
3 large eggs
⅓ cup canola oil
1 (6 ounce) package butter-brickle
    chips

1. Preheat oven to 350°.

2. Place paper baking cups in 24 muffin cups.
   Combine cake mix, eggs, oil and 1¼ cups
   water in bowl and beat on low speed for
   about 30 seconds.

3. Increase speed to medium and beat for
   2 minutes. Stir in butter-brickle chips. Fill
   muffin cups two-thirds full. Bake for 19 to
   23 minutes.

4. Cool on wire rack before removing from
   pan. Cool completely before frosting.
   Yields 24 cupcakes.

Decorations:

1 (16 ounce) container ready-to-
      serve buttercream frosting
½ cup peanut butter
24 chocolate-covered peanuts
Ground cinnamon or nutmeg

1. Place buttercream frosting in small bowl,
   stir in peanut butter and mix well.

2. Use a pastry bag (or plastic bag with a
   bottom corner cut off) fitted with a round
   tip number 8 or 10.

3. Squeeze bag evenly around cupcake
   from outside to inside. Sprinkle with
   cinnamon or nutmeg and top with
   chocolate-covered peanut.

Devil's Chocolate Cupcakes

1 (18 ounce) box devil's food cake mix
⅓ cup canola oil
3 large eggs
1 cup cold milk
1 (3.4 ounce) box instant vanilla
     pudding mix
½ cup peanut butter

1. Preheat oven to 350°.

2. Place paper baking cups in 24 muffin cups.
    Combine cake mix, oil, eggs and 1 cup
    water and beat for 2½ minutes.

3. In separate bowl, combine cold milk and
    pudding mix. Whisk for 2 minutes or until
    creamy and mixture blends well. Stir in
    peanut butter and mix well. Stir mixture
    into cake mix-eggs mixture.

4. Spoon into muffin cups and bake for
    19 to 22 minutes or until toothpick inserted
    in center comes out clean. Cool for

10 minutes in pan; cool completely before frosting. Yields 24 cupcakes.

Decorations:

1 (16 ounce) container milk chocolate frosting
Chopped nuts, butter-brickle bits or toffee bits

1. Spread chocolate frosting over cupcakes using a pastry bag (or plastic bag with a bottom corner cut off) fitted with a large star tip. Sprinkle with nuts, butter-brickle bits or toffee bits.

2. For a different look, use 1 (16 ounce) container vanilla funfetti frosting. That will give these cupcakes a "fun" look!

Rich Brownie Cupcakes

1 cup (2 sticks) unsalted butter
½ cup cocoa
½ cup sugar
1 cup packed brown sugar
3 eggs
1 teaspoon vanilla
1 cup flour
1 cup chopped pecans

1. Preheat oven to 350°.

2. Place paper baking cups in 16 muffin cups.
   Melt butter in large saucepan, stir in cocoa
   and stir until smooth. Add sugar and brown
   sugar, mix well and remove from heat.

3. Add eggs and vanilla and beat well. Stir in
   flour and pecans until they blend well. Fill
   muffin cups about three-fourths full.

4. Bake for 21 to 25 minutes or until toothpick inserted in center comes out clean. Cool completely on wire rack. Yields 16 cupcakes.

Decorations:

1 (12 ounce) container ready-to-serve chocolate frosting
1 (2 ounce) bottle candy confetti, optional

1. Use a pastry bag (or plastic bag with a bottom corner cut off) fitted with a closed star tip number 28 or 30.

2. Squeeze bag evenly around cupcake from outside to inside. Sprinkle frosting with candy confetti.

Double Rich Chocolate Cupcakes

½ cup cocoa
1⅔ cups flour
1½ cups sugar
½ teaspoon baking soda
½ cup shortening
2 eggs
1 (6 ounce) package chocolate chips

1. Preheat oven to 350°.

2. Place paper baking cups in 24 muffin cups. Mix cocoa and 1 cup hot water in bowl with spoon until mixture is smooth. Let mixture cool for about 10 minutes.

3. Add flour, sugar, baking soda, shortening and eggs and beat on low speed for 2 minutes. Increase speed and beat for additional 2 minutes. Stir in chocolate chips and mix well. Fill muffin cups half full.

4. Bake for 18 to 20 minutes or until toothpick inserted in center comes out clean. Cool completely before frosting. Yields 24 cupcakes.

Decorations:

1 (16 ounce) container ready-to-serve dark chocolate frosting
Pink sprinkles or jimmies

1. Use a pastry bag (or plastic bag with a bottom corner cut off) fitted with a closed star tip number 28 or 30.

2. Squeeze bag evenly around cupcake from outside to inside. Top with pink sprinkles.

TIP: *Grab a chocolate bar and slice chocolate curls with a potato peeler to put on top of the dark chocolate frosting. You will have Triple Chocolate Chocolate Chocolate Cupcakes!*

Double Divine Cupcakes

2 cups flour
⅔ cup cocoa
1¼ teaspoons baking soda
¾ cup (1½ sticks) unsalted butter, softened
2 cups sugar
2 large eggs, beaten
1 teaspoon vanilla
½ cup buttermilk*
½ cup chopped pecans or walnuts

1. Preheat oven to 350°.

2. Place paper baking cups in 16 muffin cups. Combine flour, cocoa, baking soda and ¼ teaspoon salt in bowl.

3. In separate bowl, beat butter and sugar until fluffy; stir in eggs and vanilla. Fold in flour mixture alternately with buttermilk and end with flour mixture. Stir in chopped pecans or walnuts.

4. Spoon into muffin cups and bake for 20 to 22 minutes or until toothpick inserted in center comes out clean. Allow to cool for 10 minutes in pan. Cool completely before frosting. Yields 16 cupcakes.

Decorations:

1 (12 ounce) container ready-to-serve milk chocolate frosting
Ground nuts

1. Use a pastry bag (or plastic bag with a bottom corner cut off) fitted with a closed star tip number 17 or 21.

2. Squeeze bag evenly around cupcake from outside to inside. Sprinkle nuts on top.

*TIP: To make buttermilk, mix 1 cup milk with 1 tablespoon lemon juice or vinegar and let milk stand for about 10 minutes.

Chocolate Fudge M&M's Cupcakes

1 (18 ounce) box triple chocolate
    fudge cake mix
3 eggs
⅓ cup canola oil
1 cup M&M's® mini chocolate
    baking bits

1. Preheat oven to 350°.

2. Place paper baking cups in 16 muffin cups.

3. Combine cake mix, eggs, oil and 1¼ cups water in bowl and beat on low speed for about 30 seconds. Increase speed to medium and beat for 2 minutes.

4. Stir in M&M's® and mix well, but gently. Fill muffin cups about two-thirds full.

5. Bake for 15 to 20 minutes. Let cool in pan for about 5 minutes. Remove from pan and let cool completely before frosting. Yields 16 cupcakes.

Decorations:

1 (16 ounce) container chocolate
    fudge frosting
½ cup very finely ground walnuts

1. Spoon chocolate fudge frosting in small
   bowl, stir in ground walnuts and mix well.

2. Spread frosting over cupcakes and be
   prepared for the chocoholics to follow the
   aroma into the kitchen.

Q. Why did the birthday cake go to the
   doctor?
A. Because it was feeling crumby!

Chocolate Round-Up Cupcakes

2 cups sugar
2 cups flour
½ cup (1 stick) butter
½ cup canola oil
4 heaping tablespoons cocoa
½ cup buttermilk*
2 eggs, beaten
1 teaspoon baking soda
1 teaspoon ground cinnamon
1 teaspoon vanilla

1. Preheat oven to 350°.

2. Place paper baking cups in 16 muffin cups. Blend sugar and flour in mixing bowl.

3. Bring butter, oil, cocoa and 1 cup water to a boil in saucepan over medium-high heat. Pour flour and sugar mixture into saucepan and beat well. Remove from heat.

4. Add buttermilk, eggs, baking soda, cinnamon, vanilla and ½ teaspoon salt. Mix well and pour into muffin cups.

5. Bake for 15 to 20 minutes until toothpick inserted in center comes out clean. Yields 16 cupcakes.

Frosting:

½ cup (1 stick) butter, melted
¼ cup cocoa
6 tablespoons milk
1 (1 pound) box powdered sugar
1 teaspoon vanilla
1 cup chopped pecans
1 (10 ounce) can flaked coconut

1. Combine butter, cocoa, milk, powdered sugar and vanilla and mix well.

2. Add pecans and coconut, mix well and spread on cupcakes.

*TIP: To make buttermilk, mix 1 cup milk with 1 tablespoon lemon juice or vinegar and let milk stand for about 10 minutes.

Chocolate-Coconut Cupcakes

2 cups flour
¾ cup sugar
3 tablespoons cocoa
1 tablespoon baking powder
1 cup milk
1 egg
⅓ cup canola oil
1½ cups flaked coconut, divided
¼ cup sweetened condensed milk
¼ teaspoon almond extract

1. Preheat oven to 350°.

2. Place paper baking cups in 14 muffin cups. Combine flour, sugar, cocoa, baking powder and ½ teaspoon salt in large bowl. In separate bowl, combine milk, egg and oil and mix well.

3. Pour milk-egg mixture into dry ingredients and stir just until moist. Spoon 2 tablespoonfuls into muffin cups.

4. Combine 1 cup coconut, sweetened condensed milk and almond extract in bowl and place 2 teaspoonfuls in center of batter of each cupcake. (Do not spread.) Top with remaining batter and sprinkle with remaining coconut.

5. Bake for 20 to 23 minutes or until toothpick inserted in cupcake comes out clean. Cool in pan for about 5 minutes.

6. Place cupcakes on wire rack to cool completely before frosting. Yields 14 cupcakes.

Decorations:

1 (12 ounce) container ready-to-serve chocolate frosting
1 (14 ounce) package sweetened flaked coconut

1. Spread frosting over each cupcake. Sprinkle coconut on top of frosting.

Cocoa-Macaroon Cupcakes

3 egg whites, divided
1 egg
⅓ cup applesauce
1 teaspoon vanilla
1¼ cups flour
1¼ cups sugar, divided
⅓ cup cocoa
½ teaspoon baking soda
¾ cup buttermilk*
1 cup ricotta cheese
1 (14 ounce) package sweetened
    flaked coconut, divided

1. Preheat oven to 350°.

2. Place paper baking cups in 18 muffin cups. Combine 2 egg whites, 1 whole egg, applesauce and vanilla in bowl.

3. In separate bowl, combine flour, 1 cup sugar, cocoa and baking soda and gradually add to egg white mixture alternately with buttermilk.

4. Place half batter into muffin cups. Beat ricotta cheese, remaining sugar and remaining egg white in bowl until mixture is smooth. Stir in half coconut.

5. Spoon 1 tablespoon ricotta mixture in center of batter in each muffin cup; fill each muffin cup with remaining batter. Bake for 26 to 30 minutes or until toothpick inserted in center comes out clean.

6. Cool for 5 minutes before removing from pan. Cool completely before frosting cupcakes. These cupcakes need to be refrigerated. Yields 18 cupcakes.

Decorations:

1 (14 ounce) container ready-to-serve caramel frosting
Remaining coconut from cupcake recipe

1. Spread thick layer of frosting over each cupcake. Sprinkle coconut on top.

TIP: To make buttermilk, mix 1 cup milk with 1 tablespoon lemon juice or vinegar and let milk stand for about 10 minutes.

Coco-Pecan Cupcakes

1 (18 ounce) box butter pecan
   cake mix
⅓ cup canola oil
3 eggs
1 (7 ounce) package flaked coconut

1. Preheat oven to 350°.

2. Place paper baking cups in 16 muffin cups. Combine cake mix, 1 cup water, oil and eggs in bowl.

3. Beat on low speed for about 30 seconds. Increase speed to medium and beat for 2 minutes.

4. Stir in coconut and pour batter into muffin cups. filling about two-thirds full.

5. Bake for 15 to 20 minutes or until toothpick inserted in center comes out clean. Cool in pan for 5 to 10 minutes. Cool completely before frosting. Yields 16 cupcakes.

Decorations:

1 (16 ounce) container
    coconut-pecan frosting
1 (2 ounce) bottle rainbow jumbo
    nonpareils
Colored candles

1. Spread coconut-pecan frosting on cupcakes and sprinkle nonpareils on top.

2. For a different decoration, use milk chocolate frosting and sprinkle with flaked coconut.

Have old memories, but young hopes.

Butter Pecan-Chocolate Cupcakes

1 (18 ounce) box butter pecan
    cake mix
⅓ cup canola oil
3 eggs
1 teaspoon butter flavoring
1 cup mini chocolate chips

1. Preheat oven to 350°.

2. Place paper baking cups in 16 muffin cups. Combine cake mix, 1¼ cups water, oil and eggs in bowl.

3. Beat on low speed for 30 seconds. Increase speed to medium and beat for 2 minutes. Stir in mini chocolate chips and spoon into 24 prepared muffin cups.

4. Bake for 15 to 20 minutes or until toothpick inserted in center comes out clean. Cool for

10 minutes in pan. Cool completely before frosting. Yields 16 cupcakes.

Decorations:

**1 (16 ounce) container milk
   chocolate frosting
1 (4 ounce) tube decorating
   white icing**

1. Spread milk chocolate frosting on each cupcake. Dip a knife in hot water and smooth the frosting surface.

2. Personalize each cupcake by making each person's initial with white decorating icing.

Favorite Afternoon Snack

1 (18 ounce) box butter pecan
    cake mix
½ cup canola oil
3 large eggs
1 teaspoon butter flavoring
1 (12 ounce) package butterscotch
    chips
½ cup finely chopped pecans

1. Preheat oven to 350°.

2. Place paper baking cups in 16 muffin cups.

3. Combine cake mix, oil, eggs, butter flavoring and 1¼ cups water in bowl and beat on low speed for about 30 seconds.

4. Increase speed to medium and beat for additional 2 minutes. Stir in butterscotch chips and mix well.

5. Pour batter into muffin cups and fill three-fourths full. Spoon 1 scant teaspoon finely chopped pecans on top of batter.

6. Bake for 15 to 20 minutes or until toothpick inserted in center comes out clean. Let cupcakes cool in pan for about 5 minutes.

7. Place cupcakes on wire rack to cool completely before frosting. Yields 16 cupcakes.

Decorations:

1 (16 ounce) container classic vanilla frosting

1. Spread frosting in a swirling motion over cupcakes. If you feel adventurous, try the coconut-pecan frosting instead of vanilla.

Sweet Toffee-Nut Cupcakes

1 (18 ounce) box pecan cake mix
⅓ cup canola oil
3 eggs
1 (14 ounce) can sweetened
    condensed milk

1. Preheat oven to 350°.

2. Place paper baking cups in 16 muffin cups.
    Combine cake mix, 1¼ cups water, oil and
    eggs in bowl.

3. Beat on low speed for 30 seconds. Increase
    speed to medium and beat for 2 minutes.

4. Pour batter into muffin cups. Bake for
    about 15 to 20 minutes until toothpick
    inserted in center comes out clean.

5. While cupcakes are still hot, poke holes
    in tops.

6. Pour sweetened condensed milk into holes, Make more holes if necessary to capture more sweetened condensed milk. Yields 16 cupcakes.

Decorations:

1 (8 ounce) carton frozen whipped
    topping, thawed
6 Heath® bars, chopped
½ cup chopped nuts

1. After cupcakes cool completely, top with whipped topping. Sprinkle chopped Heath® bars and nuts on top.

TIP: Baking times vary a lot based on size of cupcake pan, evenness of oven temperature and ingredients.

Red Velvet Cupcakes

1 (1 ounce) bottle red food coloring
1 (18 ounce) box devil's food cake mix
½ cup canola oil
3 eggs

1. Preheat oven to 350°.

2. Place paper baking cups in 16 muffin cups.
   Pour food coloring into measuring cup and
   add enough water to make 1¼ cups liquid.

3. Beat cake mix, water-food coloring mixture,
   oil and eggs in bowl.

4. Beat on low speed for 30 seconds; increase
   speed to medium and beat for 2 minutes.
   Divide batter among muffin cups.

5. Bake for 15 to 20 minutes or until toothpick
   inserted in center comes out clean. Cool
   for 10 minutes before removing from pan.
   Cool completely before frosting. Yields
   16 cupcakes.

Decorations:

1 (16 ounce) container classic
     white frosting
16 pecan halves

1. Spread white frosting over cupcakes and press 1 pecan half halfway into frosting.

2. Another way to decorate is to use 1 cup chopped pecans to cover frosting or jumbo red sprinkles over white frosting or any of the different colored Party Toppers.

Q. Why did the cook put the cake in the freezer?
A. Because she wanted icing on it!

Nutty Red Velvet Cupcakes

1 (18 ounce) box red velvet cake mix
3 eggs
⅓ cup canola oil
1 (6 ounce) package white chocolate
    chips
½ cup chopped walnuts

1. Preheat oven to 350°.

2. Place paper baking cups in 24 muffin cups. Blend cake mix, 1¼ cups water, eggs and oil in bowl on low speed for 30 seconds.

3. Beat on medium speed for 2 minutes. Stir in white chocolate chips and walnuts and pour into muffin cups.

4. Bake for 19 to 23 minutes or until toothpick inserted in center in center comes out clean. Let stand on wire rack for 30 minutes.

5. Remove each cupcake from pan and cool completely before frosting. Yields 24 cupcakes.

Decorations:

1 (16 ounce) container ready-to-serve whipped frosting

1. Use a pastry bag (or plastic bag with a bottom corner cut off) fitted with a closed star tip number 28 or 30 or just use a knife in a swirling motion.

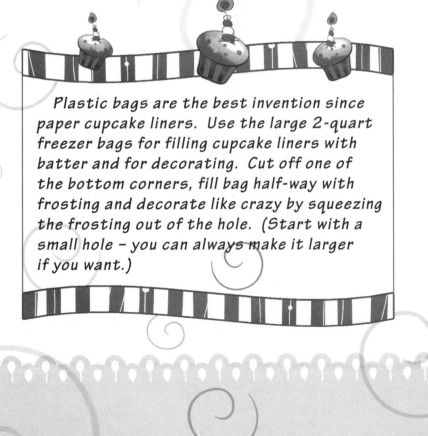

Plastic bags are the best invention since paper cupcake liners. Use the large 2-quart freezer bags for filling cupcake liners with batter and for decorating. Cut off one of the bottom corners, fill bag half-way with frosting and decorate like crazy by squeezing the frosting out of the hole. (Start with a small hole – you can always make it larger if you want.)

Angel Food Cupcakes

1 cup flour
1 cup powdered sugar
1½ cups egg whites at room
    temperature
1 teaspoon cream of tartar
1 cup sugar
1 teaspoon vanilla

1. Preheat oven to 350°.

2. Place paper baking cups in 18 muffin cups.

3. Sift flour and powdered sugar several times to make it light and airy.

4. Beat egg whites, cream of tartar and ½ teaspoon salt until thick, but not too dry.

5. Carefully fold in sugar and vanilla. Carefully fold in flour-powdered sugar mixture a little at a time.

6. Pour into muffin cups, filling about two-thirds full. Bake for 15 to 20 minutes or until toothpick inserted in center comes out clean.

7. Cool completely before frosting. Choose from frostings on pages 179-215. Yields 18 cupcakes.

TIP: *Cooking times vary with size of cupcakes. The smaller the cupcakes, the faster they cook.*

What was Snow White's brother's name? Egg White! Get the yoke?

The origin and creator of cupcakes cannot be pinpointed in culinary history, but it can be assumed that the name "cupcake" derived from its measurements.

The basic cupcake recipe started out with 1 cup butter, 1 cup sugar and 1 cup flour. This was similar to the traditional pound cake named for its measurements of 1 pound butter, 1 pound sugar, 1 pound flour and 1 pound eggs.

Another theory is that cupcakes were named for how they were baked. Instead of a large cake pan, cups and small earthenware vessels were used to make individual cakes.

The individual cake seems to be an American idea because cupcakes, as opposed to muffins, never really caught on in countries east of the Atlantic. In Europe, small cakes were not the sweet dessert treats they were in America. The term "sweet" took on a new dimension as more sugar, molasses and honey were added to baked goods in America.

Special Occasion Cupcakes

Easy Birthday Cupcakes

1 (18 ounce) box milk chocolate
    cake mix
⅓ cup canola oil
3 eggs
¼ cup chopped pecans

1. Preheat oven to 350°.

2. Place paper baking cups in 24 muffin cups.
   Combine cake mix, 1¼ cups water, oil and
   eggs in large bowl.

3. Beat on low speed for 30 seconds. Increase
   speed to medium and beat for 2 minutes.
   Stir in chopped pecans and spoon into
   muffin cups.

4. Bake for 18 to 22 minutes or until toothpick
   placed in center comes out clean.

5. Cool in pan for 5 to 10 minutes. Cool
   completely before frosting. Yields
   24 cupcakes.

Decorations:

1 (14 ounce) container ready-to-serve buttercream frosting
Candy birthday toppers or heart toppers, optional

1. Use a pastry bag (or plastic bag with a bottom corner cut off) fitted with a round tip number 7 or 10.

2. Squeeze bag evenly around cupcake from outside to inside. Place candy topper in center.

Birthdays are nature's way of telling us to eat more cake!

Birthday Chocolate Cupcakes

1 (18 ounce) box butter chocolate
    cake mix
⅓ cup canola oil
3 eggs
1 (6 ounce) package white chocolate
    chips

1. Preheat oven to 350°.

2. Place paper baking cups in 16 muffin cups. Combine cake mix, 1¼ cups water, oil and eggs in bowl and beat on low speed for 30 seconds. Increase speed to medium and beat for 2 minutes.

3. Stir in white chocolate chips. Spoon into muffin cups.

4. Bake for 15 to 20 minutes or until toothpick inserted in center comes out clean. Cool for

5 minutes before removing from pan.
Cool completely before frosting. Yields
16 cupcakes.

Decorations:

1 (16 ounce) container milk
    chocolate frosting
1 (3 ounce) bottle rainbow sprinkles
Colored candles

1. Place chocolate frosting in plastic bag, cut
   off a bottom corner and squeeze frosting
   over cupcakes in swirling motion.

2. Sprinkle a few rainbow sprinkles on each
   cupcake and top with a candle.

3. You can also buy the sugar "numbers"
   1 through 9 that can be used for the
   birthday person. Or you can add a couple
   of the "trick sparkler candles" – those will
   get attention fast!

Happy Hearts Cupcakes

1 (18 ounce) box milk chocolate
    cake mix
⅓ cup canola oil
3 eggs

1. Preheat oven to 350°.

2. Place paper baking cups in 24 muffin cups.
   Combine cake mix, 1¼ cups water, oil and
   eggs in bowl.

3. Beat on low speed for 30 seconds. Increase
   speed and beat for 2 minutes.

4. Spoon into muffin cups and bake for 19 to
   22 minutes or until toothpick inserted into
   center comes out clean.

5. Cool for 5 minutes before removing from
   pan. Cool completely before frosting.
   Yields 24 cupcakes.

Decorations:

½ cup vegetable oil
1 tablespoon egg white
2 tablespoons milk
3 cups powdered sugar
Red food coloring
Heart toppers, optional
Nonpareils, optional

1. Lightly beat vegetable oil, egg white and milk in large bowl. Add half powdered sugar and beat for a few seconds. Add remaining powdered sugar and beat on high for several minutes. (Be careful not to beat the fluff out of the frosting.)

2. Place big dollop of frosting on top of cupcake. Add one drop of red food coloring to remaining frosting and mix.

3. Place frosting in pastry bag (or plastic bag with a bottom corner cut off) fitted with an open star tip number 22 or 32. Squeeze bag to form star at very top. Decorating with heart toppers and nonpareils is optional.

Easter-Ready Cupcakes

1 (18 ounce) box yellow cake mix
⅓ cup canola oil
3 eggs

1. Preheat oven to 350°.

2. Place fancy paper baking cups in 24 muffin cups. Combine cake mix, 1¼ cups water, oil and eggs in bowl. Beat on low speed for 30 seconds.

3. Increase speed to medium and beat for 2 minutes. Spoon batter into muffin cups.

4. Bake for 19 to 22 minutes or until toothpick inserted in center comes out clean.

5. Cool in pan for 5 minutes. Cool completely before frosting. Yields 24 cupcakes.

Decorations:

1 (16 ounce) container ready-to-
    serve classic white frosting
Green food coloring
72 candy eggs

1. Place frosting in bowl. Add a drop or two
   of green food coloring and mix to get
   right color.

2. Squeeze frosting in a pattern of grass on
   each cupcake using a pastry bag (or plastic
   bag with a bottom corner cut off) fitted
   with multi-opening tip (such as Wilton
   tip #233).

3. Place 3 candy eggs in middle of grass. (Jelly
   beans would also work great.)

TIP: To make "grass" you need a thick frosting.
     Do a trial run on wax paper before you get
     started. If frosting isn't thick enough, add
     powdered sugar until the texture is right.

Fourth of July Celebration

1 (18 ounce) box yellow cake mix
⅓ cup canola oil
3 eggs
1 cup M&M's® chocolate mini
    baking bits

1. Preheat oven to 350°.

2. Place paper baking cups in 24 muffin cups.
   Combine cake mix, 1¼ cups water, oil
   and eggs in bowl and beat on low speed
   for 30 seconds.

3. Increase speed to medium and beat for
   2 minutes. Fold in M&M's® and spoon into
   muffin cups.

4. Bake for 18 to 20 minutes or until toothpick
   inserted in center comes out clean.

5. Cool for 5 to 10 minutes in pan. Cool
   completely before frosting. Yields
   24 cupcakes.

Decorations:

1 (16 ounce) container ready-to-
   serve white frosting
1 (4 ounce) bottle blue and red
   star-shaped sprinkles
2 (12 count) packages small
   sparklers

1. Spread frosting over cupcakes with a pastry
   bag (or plastic bag with a bottom corner
   cut off) fitted with a closed star tip number
   28 or 30.

2. Sprinkle generously with red and blue stars.
   Stick a small sparkler in cupcake.

Spice Up the Holidays

1 (18 ounce) box spice cake mix
1 (15 ounce) can pumpkin
3 large eggs
⅓ cup canola oil
½ teaspoon ground cinnamon
⅔ cup chopped pecans

1. Preheat oven to 350°.

2. Place paper baking cups in 24 muffin cups. Combine cake mix, pumpkin, eggs, oil, cinnamon and ⅓ cup water in bowl and beat on low speed for 30 seconds.

3. Increase speed to medium and beat for 2 minutes. Stir in chopped pecans and fill muffin cups three-fourth full with batter.

4. Bake for 19 to 23 minutes or until toothpick inserted in center comes out clean. Cool for 10 minutes before removing from pan. Cool completely before frosting. Yields 24 cupcakes.

Decorations:

1 (16 ounce) container ready-to-serve buttercream frosting
24 sugar or fondant gingerbread men, optional

1. Use a pastry bag (or plastic bag with a bottom corner cut off) fitted with an open star number 17 or 21.

2. Squeeze bag evenly around cupcake from outside to inside. Place 1 gingerbread man topper in center.

Q. What type of cake "grows" in orchards?
A. Fruit cake!

Christmas Cheer Cupcakes

1 (18 ounce) box white cake mix
⅓ cup canola oil
4 egg whites
½ cup Craisins®

1. Preheat oven to 350°.

2. Place paper baking cups in 24 muffin cups. Combine cake mix, 1¼ cups water, oil and egg whites in bowl and beat on low speed for 30 seconds.

3. Increase speed to medium and beat for 2 to 2½ minutes. Stir in Craisins® and spoon into muffin cups. (If you want the frosting to be even with the cupcake liner, only fill halfway with batter.)

4. Bake for 18 to 22 minutes or until toothpick inserted in center comes out clean.

5. Cool in pan for about 5 minutes. Remove from pan and cool completely before frosting. Yields 24 cupcakes.

Decorations:

1 (16 ounce) container ready-to-
      serve fluffy white frosting or
      white fondant
24 candy or fondant Christmas
      toppers

1. Spread white frosting smoothly over tops of
   cupcakes and add your favorite topper.

2. There are lots of "candy" figures that you
   can buy that will represent lots of themes.

3. Search for your theme in hobby, craft or
   baking supply stores and you will have a
   figure for every theme of the year.

Frosting is a mixture of sugar, butter, and water or milk and has a thick consistency so that it will hold its shape.

Icing is thinner than frosting and dries with a fairly smooth surface. It works well for decorating and is better with small holes or tips for writing.

Fondant is a type of icing that is easy to roll out, cut into shapes and mold. It will keep in the refrigerator for about two months if tightly wrapped. It is made with sugar, water and cream of tartar.

Royal icing is really good for decorations such as flowers and leaves because it will keep its shape when it dries. It is made with powdered sugar, egg whites and a little lemon juice.

Glaze is a very thin powdered sugar-water or milk mixture that is drizzled over cupcakes.

In Super Simple Cupcake Recipes we use the term frosting to include icing.

Frostings, Icings and More

Traditional Buttercream Frosting

½ cup shortening
½ cup unsalted butter
1 teaspoon vanilla
2 tablespoons milk
4 cups powdered sugar, sifted

1. Mix all ingredients until creamy. Frosting for 18 cupcakes.

TIP: *For pure white frosting, use 1 cup shortening and no butter. Add ½ teaspoon butter flavoring and 3 tablespoons corn syrup, water or milk.*

Sweet Buttercream Icing

1 (8 ounce) package cream cheese,
    softened
½ cup (1 stick) butter, softened
2 cups powdered sugar
1 teaspoon vanilla

1. Beat cream cheese and butter in bowl and
    stir in powdered sugar and vanilla. Frosting
    for 14 cupcakes.

There is a time every day when the phones go unanswered, the TV is off and e-mails can wait. For this short time, you are family and it is your dinnertime.

Decorator Frosting

2 cups powdered sugar, sifted
¼ cup plus 2 tablespoons solid
vegetable shortening, room
temperature
2 tablespoons milk
½ teaspoon almond extract
Food coloring

1. Beat powdered sugar, shortening, milk, almond extract and pinch of salt in bowl on low speed until smooth and creamy.

2. Start with 1 small drop of your favorite food coloring. Add more if needed for deeper color. Frosting for 24 cupcakes.

December 16th is National Chocolate-Covered Anything Day!

Fondant

2½ cups sugar
1 cup water
⅛ teaspoon cream of tartar

1. Combine ingredients. Heat to the boiling point, stirring until sugar dissolves.

2. Continue boiling, brushing syrup form sides of pan until the temperature reaches (238° on a candy thermometer) or until a small amount dropped into cold water will form a soft ball.

3. Remove to shallow dish. When lukewarm, stir until white and creamy. Add any desired flavoring or coloring. Cool.

4. When ready to use for icing, warm slightly over hot water.

TIP: Remember, a little food coloring goes a long way. Always start with only a drop or two. Add more if you want a deeper color.

Ornamental Icing

1 egg white
2¾ cups confectioners' sugar
½ teaspoon lemon juice

1. Beat egg with 1 cup sugar until stiff. Add lemon juice and beat in.

2. Add remaining sugar, a small amount at a time, beating after each addition. Cool.

3. Any desired food coloring may be beaten into this icing.

TIP: When this icing dries, it hardens; it is good for making decorations.

Quick Icing

1 cup sugar
1 egg white
½ teaspoon vanilla

1. Put sugar, ¼ cup water and egg white in saucepan and cook over boiling water.

2. Beat constantly until frosting is the proper consistency to spread. Add vanilla. Icing for 14 cupcakes.

TIP: This icing dries hard and is good for making decorations.

Sprinkle powdered sugar over top of cupcake before icing to keep icing in place.

Brown Sugar Icing

½ cup (1 stick) unsalted butter
1 cup packed brown sugar
¼ cup milk
1¾ - 2 cups powdered sugar
½ teaspoon vanilla

1. Melt butter in heavy saucepan, add brown sugar and milk and cook for about 3 minutes, stirring constantly. Cool for 10 minutes.

2. Add 1¾ cups powdered sugar and vanilla; beat until creamy. If needed, add more powdered sugar to make spreadable consistency. Frosting for 24 cupcakes.

Champion Cream Frosting

¾ cup (1½ sticks) unsalted butter, softened
⅓ cup sour cream
4 - 4½ cups powdered sugar, sifted
1 teaspoon vanilla

1. Beat butter, sour cream and pinch of salt in bowl until creamy. Gradually add 4 cups powdered sugar and beat until light and fluffy.

2. Add more powdered sugar if needed for spreading consistency.

3. Stir in vanilla and mix well. Refrigerate. Frosting for 24 cupcakes.

Creamy 2-Layer Cake Icing

¾ cup (1½ sticks) butter, softened
1½ (8 ounce) packages cream
    cheese, softened
1 teaspoon vanilla
1½ teaspoons almond extract
1½ - 2 (1 pound) boxes powdered
    sugar

1. Beat butter and cream cheese in bowl until they blend well and are smooth.

2. Stir in vanilla and almond extract and gradually add as much powdered sugar as needed for spreading evenly over layers and sides of cake.

Rich Vanilla Frosting

1¼ cups (2½ sticks) unsalted
    butter, softened
2 tablespoons whipping cream
1 teaspoon vanilla
2½ - 2¾ cups powdered sugar

1. Beat butter in bowl on medium-high speed for about 1 minute or until smooth

2. Stir in cream, vanilla and a pinch of salt and mix well.

3. Reduce speed to medium-low and gradually add powdered sugar; beat until mixture is light and fluffy. Refrigerate. Frosting for 24 cupcakes.

Velvet Whipped Cream Frosting

1½ cups whipping cream
3 tablespoons cocoa
5 tablespoons powdered sugar
½ teaspoon vanilla

1. Beat cream, cocoa, powdered sugar and vanilla in bowl on medium-high speed until soft peaks form.

2. Refrigerate. Frosting for 14 to 15 cupcakes.

Let butter come to room temperature before using it. The texture of the product will be better if it is soft than if you mix cold butter or melted butter with ingredients.

Dark Chocolate Frosting

1¼ cups (2½ sticks) unsalted
    butter, softened
8 (1 ounce) squares semi-sweet
    chocolate, melted
1 teaspoon vanilla
1 (16 ounce) box powdered sugar
2 tablespoons cocoa

1. Beat butter in bowl on medium speed until smooth. Stir in melted chocolate, vanilla and pinch of salt.

2. In separate bowl, combine powdered sugar and cocoa. Gradually add sugar-cocoa mixture to butter mixture and beat until light and fluffy. Frosting for 24 cupcakes.

A Brownie Frosting

2 tablespoons butter
2 (1 ounce) squares unsweetened
 chocolate
2 tablespoons strong brewed coffee,
 warm
2 teaspoons milk
2 teaspoons vanilla
1 (1 pound) box powdered sugar,
 sifted

1. Melt butter and chocolate in heavy
   saucepan and stir well.

2. Add coffee, milk and vanilla, stir and
   remove from heat.

3. Whisk in powdered sugar and beat until
   smooth. If frosting is too thick to spread,
   thin with a little bit more milk.

4. Spread over pan of brownies, bars or
   squares. Frosting for 15 to 20 cupcakes.

Creamy Chocolate Frosting

¼ cup shortening, melted
⅔ cup cocoa
⅓ cup milk
2 teaspoons vanilla
3 - 3½ cups powdered sugar, sifted

1. Combine shortening, cocoa, milk and a pinch of salt in bowl; mix until they blend well.

2. Add about 1 cup powdered sugar at a time and mix well after each addition.

3. More powdered sugar may be needed to thicken mixture or a little more milk may be needed to thin it.

4. Stir until frosting is right consistency to spread over cake. Frosting for 18 to 20 cupcakes or 1 (2 layer) cake or 1 (9 x 13-inch) cake.

Quick Chocolate Frosting

½ cup (1 stick) butter
¼ cup plus 2 tablespoons cream
3 tablespoons cocoa
4 cups powdered sugar
1 teaspoon vanilla

1. Combine butter, cream and cocoa in saucepan; stir and bring to a boil.

2. Remove from heat and slowly whisk in powdered sugar and vanilla until smooth. Frosting for about 26 cupcakes.

The U.S. produces more chocolate than any other country, but the Swiss consume the most followed closely by the English.

Kahlua-Chocolate Frosting

¼ cup (½ stick) unsalted butter,
    softened
1 (8 ounce) package cream cheese,
    softened
1 (16 ounce) box powdered sugar,
    sifted, divided
2 (1 ounce) squares unsweetened
    chocolate, melted, cooled
¼ cup Kahlua® liqueur*

1. Beat butter and cream cheese in bowl until creamy. Add 1 cup powdered sugar and melted chocolate and beat until creamy.

2. Gradually add remaining powdered sugar and Kahlua®. Beat on low speed until spreading consistency. Refrigerate. Frosting for 24 cupcakes.

*TIP: If you don't want to use Kahlua®, just use ¼ cup strong, brewed coffee instead.

Creamy Mocha Icing

1 tablespoon instant coffee granules
½ cup (1 stick) unsalted butter,
    softened
3 tablespoons cocoa
4¼ cups powdered sugar, sifted,
    divided
1 teaspoon vanilla

1. Dissolve coffee granules in ¼ cup hot water and let cool for about 10 minutes.

2. Beat butter and cocoa in bowl on medium speed until creamy.

3. Gradually add 4 cups powdered sugar alternately with coffee mixture, beginning and ending with powdered sugar.

4. Add more powdered sugar if needed for spreading consistency. Stir in vanilla and mix well. Frosting for 24 cupcakes.

Sweet Coffee-Cocoa Icing

½ cup (1 stick) unsalted butter
¾ cup cocoa
¼ cup cold brewed coffee
1 teaspoon vanilla
1 (16 ounce) box powdered sugar

1. Beat butter in bowl on medium speed until very light.

2. Stir in cocoa, coffee, vanilla, a pinch of salt and powdered sugar; blend thoroughly. Frosting for 24 cupcakes.

TIP: *If you want a stronger coffee flavor, stir about 1 or 2 tablespoons instant coffee granules into the brewed coffee.*

Chocolate-Java Frosting

¼ cup (½ stick) butter, softened
1 (8 ounce) package cream cheese, softened
1 (16 ounce) box powdered sugar, sifted, divided
2 (1 ounce) squares unsweetened chocolate, melted, cooled
¼ cup strong brewed coffee

1. Beat butter and cream cheese in bowl until creamy.

2. Add 1 cup powdered sugar and melted chocolate and beat until creamy.

3. Gradually add remaining powdered sugar and brewed coffee. Beat on low speed until spreading consistency. Refrigerate. Frosting for 24 cupcakes.

Golden Halo Coconut Frosting

2 tablespoons whipping cream
1 teaspoon coconut extract
1 teaspoon vanilla
1 cup (2 sticks) unsalted butter, softened
¼ cup cream of coconut
3 cups powdered sugar
¼ cup shredded coconut, toasted

1. In bowl, combine cream, coconut extract, vanilla and pinch of salt. In mixing bowl, beat butter and cream of coconut at medium to high speed until smooth.

2. Reduce speed to medium-low, slowly add powdered sugar and beat until smooth. Increase speed to high and beat until mixture is light and fluffy, about 5 minutes.

3. Frost cupcakes and sprinkle tops with toasted coconut. Frosting for 14 cupcakes.

TIP: To toast coconut, bake in shallow pan for about 5 minutes at 300°. Watch closely because coconut will burn easily.

Completely Coco-Nutty Icing

1½ cups sugar
6 tablespoons (¾ stick) butter
1 cup sweetened condensed milk
1 cup chopped pecans
1 cup flaked coconut

1. Combine sugar, butter and sweetened condensed milk in saucepan and bring to a boil.

2. Boil for 2 minutes and stir in pecans and coconut. Icing for 14 cupcakes.

Q. Did you hear somebody robbed the bakery yesterday?
A. Doesn't that take the cake!

Pecan-Coconut 2-Layer Cake Icing

1½ cups sugar
½ cup (1 stick) butter
1 (5 ounce) can evaporated milk
1 cup chopped pecans
1 (3 ounce) can flaked coconut
1 teaspoon vanilla

1. Combine sugar, butter and evaporated milk in saucepan, boil for 4 minutes and stir constantly.

2. Remove from heat and add pecans, coconut and vanilla. Spread over hot cupcakes, cake, bars or squares. Icing for 14 cupcakes.

Hot 'n Creamy Crunch Icing

6 tablespoons milk
½ cup (1 stick) butter
⅓ cup cocoa
1 (1 pound) box powdered sugar
1 teaspoon vanilla
½ cup chopped pecans

1. Combine milk, butter and cocoa in saucepan, bring to a boil over medium heat; stir often.

2. Remove from heat, stir in powdered sugar and vanilla until smooth. Add pecans and mix well. Icing for 14 cupcakes.

Peanut Butter Icing

2 cups powdered sugar
3 tablespoons peanut butter
1 teaspoon cinnamon
1 teaspoon nutmeg
4 - 6 tablespoons milk

1. Combine all ingredients except milk.

2. Add milk slowly until right consistency to spread. Frosting for 18 cupcakes.

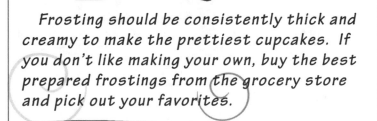

Frosting should be consistently thick and creamy to make the prettiest cupcakes. If you don't like making your own, buy the best prepared frostings from the grocery store and pick out your favorites.

Nutty Buttercream Icing

1 (3 ounce) package cream cheese, softened
6 tablespoons (¾ stick) unsalted butter, softened
1 tablespoon milk
1 teaspoon vanilla
2 cups powdered sugar
½ cup chopped pecans

1. Beat cream cheese and butter in bowl. Stir in milk, vanilla, powdered sugar and pecans. Frosting for 18 cupcakes.

Q. What cake is as hard as rock?
A. Marble cake!

Deluxe Cream Cheese Frosting

1 (8 ounce) package cream cheese, softened
½ cup (1 stick) unsalted butter, softened
1 (16 ounce) box powdered sugar
¾ teaspoon almond extract
1½ cups chopped pecans

1. Beat cream cheese and butter in bowl on medium speed until smooth and creamy.

2. Reduce speed to low, gradually add powdered sugar and beat until light and fluffy.

3. Stir in almond extract and pecans. Refrigerate. Frosting for 24 cupcakes.

Caramel Icing

2 cups packed brown sugar
1 cup sugar
1 cup sour cream or milk
1 tablespoon unsalted butter
1 teaspoon vanilla
Cream

1. Combine sugar, brown sugar and sour cream in large saucepan and cook slowly until sugars dissolve.

2. Cook until a little of the mixture dropped in cold water forms soft ball (238° on candy thermometer).

3. Remove from heat, add butter and vanilla, and cool to 145° or until outside of saucepan feels warm to the touch.

4. Beat until quite stiff, then add enough cream while beating to make spreading consistency. Frosting for 18 cupcakes.

Marshmallow Heaven Icing

1 cup (2 sticks) butter, softened
1 (7 ounce) jar marshmallow creme
2 cups powdered sugar
1 teaspoon vanilla

1. Beat all ingredients in bowl until they blend. Increase speed to high and continue beating for additional 2 minutes until smooth and fluffy. Icing for 14 cupcakes.

You can freeze cupcakes for up to three months. Decorated cupcakes don't freeze as well, but you can always freeze the cupcakes and spread icing and apply decorations later.

Powdered Sugar Glaze

1 cup sifted powdered sugar
1 tablespoon plus 1 teaspoon milk
½ teaspoon vanilla

1. In mixing bowl, beat powdered sugar, milk and vanilla on medium speed until smooth and creamy.

2. This glaze is good for the top of pound cakes. Yields ½ cup.

TIP: For orange glaze, substitute orange juice for milk

Q: How do chickens bake a cake?
A: From scratch!

Sweet Glaze Drizzle

1 cup sugar
1½ teaspoons baking soda
½ cup buttermilk*
½ cup (1 stick) butter
2 tablespoons light corn syrup
1 teaspoon vanilla

1. In large, heavy saucepan, combine sugar, baking soda, buttermilk, butter and corn syrup and bring to a boil. Boil 4 minutes, stirring constantly until glaze is golden.

2. Remove from heat and sir in vanilla. This is best drizzled over a cake and letting some run down sides of cake. Yields 1½ cups

*TIP: To make buttermilk, mix 1 cup milk with 1 tablespoon lemon juice or vinegar and let milk stand for about 10 minutes.

Fudge Glaze

1 (1 ounce) square unsweetened
    chocolate
3 tablespoons butter
1 - 1¼ cups powdered sugar
1 teaspoon vanilla
2 - 3 tablespoons warm milk

1. Melt chocolate and butter in large saucepan. Blend in powdered sugar (more if needed) and vanilla with whisk.

2. Add just enough milk to make smooth, spreadable glaze.

3. Yields glaze for about 14 cupcakes or 1 (9 x 13-inch) cake or pan of brownies or squares.

Spiced Whipped Cream

1 cup whipping cream
3 tablespoons powdered sugar
1 teaspoon cinnamon
1 teaspoon ginger

1. Whip cream until stiff and add sugar and spices.

Maybe the little things, like having a meal at the table, are more important than we realize. Maybe these little things are really big things we never forget...big things like memories and family traditions that last a lifetime.

Dutch Apple-Nut Crumble Topping

½ cup packed brown sugar
2 tablespoons unsalted butter, softened
2 tablespoons flour
Dash ground nutmeg
Dash ground cinnamon
½ - ¾ cup chopped nuts

1. Cream brown sugar and butter, add remaining ingredients and mix well.

2. Crumble over top of cupcakes while still hot. Tops 18 cupcakes.

Q. What do you call a stolen Hershey® bar?
A. Hot chocolate!

Creamy Lemon Filling

1 (14 ounce) can sweetened
    condensed milk
2 teaspoons grated lemon peel
Scant ⅓ cup lemon juice
¼ teaspoon vanilla
2 - 4 drops yellow food coloring
1½ cups frozen whipped topping,
    thawed

1. Combine sweetened condensed milk,
   lemon peel, lemon juice, vanilla and
   2 drops food coloring. Stir well with
   wire whisk.

2. Slowly fold in whipped topping and
   mix until it blends well.

3. Add more food coloring if desired.
   Refrigerate. Yields 3 cups.

Old-Fashioned Cream Filling

⅓ cup flour
⅔ cup sugar
2 cups milk
2 tablespoons butter
3 egg yolks, beaten
½ tablespoon vanilla

1. Mix flour, sugar and ¼ teaspoon salt. Scald milk and slowly add to dry mixture while stirring.

2. Place saucepan in larger pan half filled with hot water and stir until thick, about 15 minutes.

3. Add butter and stir to melt. Pour mixture over egg yolks; stir constantly. Cool slightly before adding vanilla.

Marshmallow Cream Filling

¾ cup sugar
⅓ cup corn syrup
16 marshmallows, cut in quarters
2 egg whites, stiffly beaten

1. Cook sugar, corn syrup and ¼ cup water together in a saucepan until it spins a long thread (240° on candy thermometer) when dropped from a metal spoon.

2. Remove from heat and immediately add marshmallows. Beat until thoroughly blended.

3. Pour the hot syrup over the egg whites and continue betting until mixture is smooth. Yields 1½ to 2 cups.

Because the ingredients were expensive to buy, cake itself was considered to be a rich man's food in early America. After the American Industrial Revolution took place between the years of 1780 and 1860, baking ingredients were easier to come by and became more affordable for common folk.

Teacake is a generic term for cookies, breads, muffins or cakes. People ate them while "taking tea" in an age when people had time to "take tea" in the middle of the afternoon.

Bonus Section:

EASY CAKES!

Easy Applesauce-Spice Cake

1 (18 ounce) box spice cake mix
3 eggs
1¼ cups applesauce
⅓ cup canola oil
1 cup chopped walnuts

1. Preheat oven to 350°.

2. Beat cake mix, eggs, applesauce and oil in bowl on medium speed for 2 minutes. Stir in walnuts.

3. Pour into sprayed, floured 9 x 13-inch baking pan.

4. Bake for 40 minutes. Cake is done when toothpick inserted in center comes out clean. Cool completely.

Frosting:

1 (16 ounce) container vanilla
    frosting
½ teaspoon ground cinnamon

1. Combine icing and cinnamon and spread
    over cake. Serves 12 to 14.

To avoid crumbs in frosting, dust the top of cupcakes or cakes with your finger to remove loose crumbs. Spread a thin layer of frosting before putting the final layer of frosting down to avoid crumbs resurfacing. Wash knife with hot water when too much frosting sticks to it.

Chocolate Hurricane Cake

This is easy and very, very yummy!

1 cup chopped pecans
1 (3 ounce) can sweetened flaked
   coconut
1 (18 ounce) box German chocolate
   cake mix
1¼ cups water
⅓ cup canola oil
3 eggs
½ cup (1 stick) butter, melted
1 (8 ounce) package cream cheese,
   softened
1 (16 ounce) box powdered sugar

1. Preheat oven to 350°.

2. Cover bottom of sprayed 9 x 13-inch baking
   pan with pecans and coconut.

3. In mixing bowl, combine cake mix, water, oil and eggs and beat well. Carefully pour batter over pecans and coconut.

4. In mixing bowl, combine butter, cream cheese and powdered sugar and whip to blend.

5. Spoon mixture over batter and bake for 40 to 42 minutes. (You cannot test for doneness with toothpick because cake will appear sticky even when it is done.)

6. The topping sinks into bottom as it bakes and forms white ribbon inside.

What happened to the lazy employee at the gum factory? He got chewed out!

Chocolate Pudding Cake

1 (18 ounce) box milk chocolate
    cake mix
1¼ cups milk
⅓ cup canola oil
3 eggs

1. Preheat oven to 350°.

2. Combine all ingredients in bowl and beat well.

3. Pour into sprayed 9 x 13-inch baking pan.

4. Bake for 35 minutes or until toothpick inserted in center comes out clean.

Topping:

1 (14 ounce) can sweetened
    condensed milk
¾ (16 ounce) can chocolate syrup
1 (8 ounce) carton frozen whipped
    topping, thawed
⅓ cup chopped pecans

1. Mix sweetened condensed milk and
   chocolate syrup in small bowl.

2. Pour over cake and let soak into cake.
   Refrigerate for several hours.

3. Spread whipped topping over top of cake
   and sprinkle pecans on top. Refrigerate
   before serving. Serves 16 to 18.

Chocolate Turtle Cake

1 (18 ounce) box German chocolate
　　cake mix
½ cup (1 stick) butter, softened
1½ cups water
½ cup oil
1 (14 ounce) can sweetened,
　　condensed milk, divided
1 (1 pound) bag caramels
1 cup chopped pecans

1. Preheat oven to 350°.

2. Combine cake mix, butter, water, oil and
   half condensed milk. Pour half batter
   into sprayed 9 x 13-inch pan and bake
   for 20 minutes.

3. Melt caramels and blend with remaining
   condensed milk. Spread evenly over baked
   cake layer and sprinkle with pecans.

4. Cover with remaining batter and bake an
   additional 20 to 25 minutes.

Icing:

½ cup (1 stick) butter
3 tablespoons cocoa
6 tablespoons evaporated milk
1 (16 ounce) box powdered sugar
1 teaspoon vanilla

1. Melt butter in saucepan and mix in cocoa and milk. Remove from heat.

2. Add powdered sugar and vanilla to mixture and blend well. Spread over cake. Serves 24.

Pound cake was given its name because the original recipe called for one pound of butter, one pound of sugar, one pound of flour and one pound of eggs (about eight large).

Great Coconut Cake Deluxe

This cake is really moist and delicious and can be frozen if you need to make it in advance.

1 (18 ounce) box yellow cake mix
3 eggs
⅓ cup canola oil
1 (14 ounce) can sweetened,
    condensed milk
1 (15 ounce) can cream of coconut
1 (8 ounce) carton frozen whipped
    topping, thawed
1 (3 ounce) can flaked coconut

1. Preheat oven to 350°.

2. Prepare cake mix according to package directions with eggs, oil and 1¼ cups water.

3. Pour into sprayed 9 x 13-inch baking pan. Bake for 30 to 35 minutes or until toothpick inserted in center comes out clean.

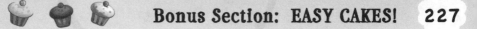

4. While cake is warm, punch holes in cake about 2 inches apart.

5. Pour condensed milk over cake and spread around until all milk soaks into cake. Pour cream of coconut over cake.

6. Cool and frost with whipped topping. Sprinkle coconut over top. Serves 12 to 15.

Mixers in a stand beat faster than handheld mixers. Don't over-mix if you use a stand mixer when the recipe calls for a hand mixer.

Favorite Cake

1 (18 ounce) box butter pecan
    cake mix
3 eggs
⅓ cup canola oil
1 cup almond toffee bits
1 cup chopped pecans
Powdered sugar, sifted

1. Preheat oven to 350°.

2. Mix cake mix with eggs, oil and 1¼ cups water according to package directions. Fold in toffee bits and pecans.

3. Pour into sprayed, floured bundt cake pan. Bake for 45 minutes or until toothpick inserted in center comes out clean.

4. Allow cake to cool for several minutes and remove cake from pan. Dust with sifted powdered sugar. Serves 18.

Mom's Pound Cake

1 cup (2 sticks) butter, softened
2 cups sugar
5 eggs
2 cups flour
1 tablespoon almond extract

1. Preheat oven to 325°.

2. Combine all ingredients in mixing bowl and beat for 10 minutes at medium speed. (Batter will be very thick.)

3. Pour into sprayed, floured tube pan.

4. Bake for 1 hour. Cake is done when toothpick inserted in center comes out clean.

The Best Fresh Apple Cake

1½ cups canola oil
2 cups sugar
3 eggs
2½ cups sifted flour
½ teaspoon salt
1 teaspoon baking soda
2 teaspoons baking powder
½ teaspoon cinnamon
1 teaspoon vanilla
3 cups peeled, grated apples
1 cup chopped pecans

1. Preheat oven to 350°.

2. Mix oil, sugar and eggs and beat well.

3. In separate bowl, sift flour, salt, baking soda, baking powder and cinnamon.

4. Gradually add flour mixture to cream mixture.

5. Add vanilla and fold in apples and pecans and pour into sprayed tube pan. Bake for 1 hour.

6. Remove from oven, cool and invert onto serving plate.

Glaze:

2 tablespoons (¼ stick) butter, melted
2 tablespoons milk
1 cup powdered sugar
1 teaspoon vanilla
¼ teaspoon lemon extract

1. Mix all ingredients and drizzle over cake.

Ralph: Did you hear the joke about the broken egg?
Eddie: Yes, it cracked me up!

Miracle Cake

1 (18 ounce) box lemon cake mix
3 eggs
⅓ cup canola oil
1 (20 ounce) can crushed pineapple
    with juice

1. Preheat oven to 350°.

2. Combine all ingredients in bowl.

3. Blend on low speed and beat on medium for 2 minutes.

4. Pour batter into sprayed, floured 9 x 13-inch baking pan.

5. Bake for 30 to 35 minutes or until toothpick inserted in center comes out clean.

Miracle Cake Topping:

1 (14 ounce) can sweetened
    condensed milk
¼ cup lemon juice
1 (8 ounce) carton frozen whipped
    topping, thawed

1. Blend all ingredients in bowl and mix well.
   Spread over cake. Refrigerate. Serves 18.

We hope everyone recognizes the importance of sharing time and meals together. If you do, our families will be stronger, our nation will be stronger and our own little part of the world will feel a little safer and a little more loving. The Publisher

Old-Fashioned Carrot Cake

1 (10 ounce) package shredded
    carrots
2 cups flour
1 teaspoon baking soda
1 teaspoon baking powder
2 cups sugar
1 teaspoon ground cinnamon
4 eggs, beaten
¾ cup oil
1 teaspoon vanilla

1. Preheat oven to 350°.

2. Combine carrots, flour, baking soda,
   baking powder, ½ teaspoon salt, sugar and
   cinnamon in bowl.

3. Add eggs, oil and vanilla and stir until
   blended.

4. Pour batter into three sprayed, wax paper-
   lined 9-inch round cake pans.

5. Bake for 25 minutes or until toothpick inserted in center comes out clean. Cool in pans for 10 minutes. Remove and cool completely on wire racks.

Cream Cheese Frosting:

1 (8 ounce) package cream cheese
½ cup (1 stick) butter
1 (16 ounce) box powdered sugar
1 teaspoon vanilla

1. Beat cream cheese and butter at medium speed until fluffy.

2. Gradually add sugar and beat well.

3. Stir in vanilla.

4. Spread frosting between layers and on top and sides of cooled cake.

Oreo Cake

1 (18 ounce) box white cake mix
⅓ cup canola oil
4 egg whites
1¼ cup coarsely chopped Oreo®
    cookies

1. Preheat oven to 350°.

2. Combine cake mix, oil, egg whites and 1¼ cups water in bowl.

3. Blend on low speed until moist and then beat for 2 minutes on high speed.

4. Gently fold in coarsely chopped cookies and pour batter into 2 sprayed, floured 8-inch round cake pans.

5. Bake for 25 to 30 minutes or until toothpick inserted in center comes out clean.

6. Cool for 15 minutes and remove from pan. Cool completely before frosting.

Frosting:

4¼ cups powdered sugar
1 cup (2 sticks) butter, softened
1 cup shortening*
1 teaspoon almond extract
½ cup crushed Oreo® cookies

1. Combine all ingredients except crushed cookies in bowl and beat until creamy.

2. Frost first layer of cake, place second layer on top and frost top and sides.

3. Sprinkle cookie crumbs over top.

*TIP: Do not use butter-flavored shortening.

When asked what is the meaning of life, the old woman quickly answered, "Chocolate".

Pineapple Upside-Down Cake

½ cup (1 stick) butter
2 cups packed light brown sugar
1 (20 ounce) can crushed pineapple,
    drained
10 maraschino cherries, quartered
1 (18 ounce) box pineapple cake mix
3 eggs
⅓ cup canola oil

1. Preheat oven to 350°.

2. In small saucepan, melt butter and brown sugar until creamy.

3. Divide mixture evenly between 2 sprayed, floured 9-inch cake pans.

4. Spread pineapple and cherries evenly over brown sugar mixture in each pan.

5. Prepare cake batter according to package directions with eggs, oil and 1¼ cups water and pour over pineapple.

6. Bake for 35 to 40 minutes or until toothpick inserted in center of cake comes out clean.

7. Remove cake from oven and cool for 10 minutes.

8. Put plate on top of cake pan, turn cake pan upside down and tap bottom of cake pan several times with knife. Gently lift cake pan off cake.

Q. Why did Susan stand on her head at the birthday party?
A. They were having upside-down cake!

Old-Fashioned White Cake with Chocolate Frosting

½ cup (1 stick) butter, softened
1⅛ cups sugar
1 teaspoon vanilla
⅔ cup milk, beaten
3 egg whites, beaten
2 cups flour
2½ teaspoons baking powder

1. Preheat oven to 350°.

2. Beat butter and sugar until they mix well. Add vanilla, milk and beaten egg whites and beat until they mix well.

3. In separate bowl, mix flour, baking powder and ½ teaspoon salt.

4. Gradually pour flour mixture into butter mixture a little at a time; stir after each addition.

5. Pour batter into 2 sprayed 8-inch cake pans.

6. Bake for 25 minutes or until toothpick inserted in center comes out clean. Cool before frosting.

Creamy Chocolate Frosting

4 (1 ounce) squares baking chocolate
¾ cup packed brown sugar
¼ cup (½ stick) butter
2 cups powdered sugar
2 egg yolks
¾ teaspoon vanilla

1. Combine chocolate, brown sugar, butter, ⅓ cup water and ¼ teaspoon salt in saucepan over medium heat. Stir until chocolate and butter melt.

2. Simmer for 2 to 3 additional minutes to mix ingredients well or until frosting begins to thicken.

3. Add powdered sugar a little at a time and beat after each addition.

4. Add egg yolks and vanilla and beat until ingredients blend well and frosting is smooth.

Pan Sizes and Batter Amounts

Pan Size	Batter Amount	Estimated Baking Time @ 350°
Standard Muffin Pan	¼ to ⅓ cup per cupcake	18 to 20 minutes
Mini-Muffin Pan	1 heaping tablespoon	8 to 10 minutes
Jumbo Muffin Pan	½ to ⅔ cup	20 to 22 minutes
King-size Muffin Pan	⅞ cup	24 to 26 minutes

The best way to fill cupcake liners with batter is with an ice cream scoop or a melon baller for bite-size cupcakes.

Dark pans may cause cupcakes to cook a little faster or look a little darker. Shiny pans are best.

To keep cleanup to a minimum, use paper liners inside each cupcake mold. They also help keep cupcakes from drying out. Plus, their color is a decoration!

Silicone muffin/cupcake pans are great for easy cleanup and longevity. Place them on a cookie sheet and make sure it is level.

Index

A

B

C

N

Cookbooks Published by Cookbook Resources, LLC
Bringing Family and Friends to the Table

The Best 1001 Short, Easy Recipes

1001 Slow Cooker Recipes

1001 Short, Easy, Inexpensive Recipes

1001 Fast Easy Recipes

1001 Community Recipes

Easy Slow Cooker Cookbook

Busy Woman's Slow Cooker Recipes

Busy Woman's Quick & Easy Recipes

Easy Diabetic Recipes

365 Easy Soups and Stews

365 Easy Chicken Recipes

365 Easy One-Dish Recipes

365 Easy Soup Recipes

365 Easy Vegetarian Recipes

365 Easy Casserole Recipes

365 Easy Pasta Recipes

365 Easy Slow Cooker Recipes

Super Simple Cupcake Recipes

Leaving Home Cookbook and Survival Guide

Essential 3-4-5 Ingredient Recipes

Ultimate 4 Ingredient Cookbook

Easy Cooking with 5 Ingredients

The Best of Cooking with 3 Ingredients

Ultimate 4 Ingredient Diabetic Cookbook

4-Ingredient Recipes for 30-Minute Meals

Cooking with Beer

The Pennsylvania Cookbook

The California Cookbook

Best-Loved New England Recipes

Best-Loved Canadian Recipes

Best-Loved Recipes from the Pacific Northwest

Easy Slow Cooker Recipes (with Photos)

Cool Smoothies (with Photos)

Easy Cupcake Recipes (with Photos)

Easy Soup Recipes (with Photos)

Classic Tex-Mex and Texas Cooking

Best-Loved Southern Recipes

Classic Southwest Cooking

Miss Sadie's Southern Cooking

Classic Pennsylvania Dutch Cooking

Healthy Cooking with 4 Ingredients

Trophy Hunters' Wild Game Cookbook

Recipe Keeper

Simple Old-Fashioned Baking

Quick Fixes with Cake Mixes

Kitchen Keepsakes & More Kitchen Keepsakes

Cookbook 25 Years

Texas Longhorn Cookbook

Gifts for the Cookie Jar

All New Gifts for the Cookie Jar

The Big Bake Sale Cookbook

Easy One-Dish Meals

Easy Potluck Recipes

Easy Casseroles Cookbook

Easy Desserts

Sunday Night Suppers

Easy Church Suppers

365 Easy Meals

Gourmet Cooking with 5 Ingredients

Muffins In A Jar

A Little Taste of Texas

A Little Taste of Texas II

cookbook *resources* LLC

www.cookbookresources.com

Toll-Free 866-229-2665

Your Ultimate Source for Easy Cookbooks

Cool Smoothies

Beautiful 4-color photographs complement the world of smoothies – simple to make and enjoy! So attractive and easy-to-use, it's also a great gift.

Size 4⅛ x 7   176 pages

Hard Cover
Concealed Wire-O